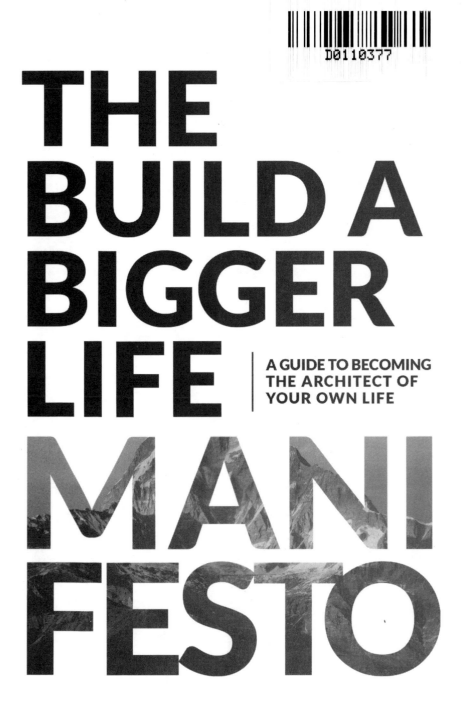

THE BUILD A BIGGER LIFE

A GUIDE TO BECOMING THE ARCHITECT OF YOUR OWN LIFE

MANI FESTO

THE BUILD A BIGGER LIFE MANFESTO

A GUIDE TO BECOMING THE ARCHITECT OF YOUR OWN LIFE

To A BIGGER LIFE!

ADAM CARROLL

BookPress®

www.BookpressPublishing.com

Published in Des Moines, Iowa, by:

BookPress Publishing
P.O. Box 71532, Des Moines, IA 50325
www.BookpressPublishing.com

Publisher's Cataloging-in-Publication Data

Names: Carroll, Adam Paul, author.
Title: The Build a Bigger Life Manifesto : The guide to becoming the architect of your own life / Adam Carroll.
Description: Includes bibliographical records. | Des Moines, IA: BookPress Publishing, 2020.
Identifiers: LCCN: 2020901112 | ISBN: 978-1-947305-13-7
Subjects: LCSH Success. | Self-Actualization (Psychology) | Conduct of life. | Leadership. | BISAC SELF-HELP / Personal Growth / Success
Classification: LCC BF637.S8 C3756 2020 | DDC 158.1--dc23

First Edition
Printed in the United States of America
10 9 8 7 6 5 4 3 2 1

*This book is dedicated to those who yearn for
a life bigger than what they are currently living,
but aren't sure how to go after it. May you always
see yourself as the architect of your own life!*

CONTENTS

ACKNOWLEDGEMENTS

Thanks to the life architects who have joined me on the Build a Bigger Life podcast through the years. You are shining examples of what it takes to hold bigger visions and ask bigger questions.

Introduction

Tenet (Noun)

A principle or belief, especially one of the
main principles of a religion or philosophy.

Several years ago, someone inspired me to begin writing
a manifesto to my children, a guidebook of sorts to living a
life that filled them up rather than one that depleted them.

I began curating tidbits of advice, articles, and books
that would help my children. The information I started
capturing was equal parts "what to do" and "what not to do,"
and, eventually, the advice started to take shape into concrete
ideas and actionable items. I spent two years interviewing
successful, passionate people both in person and on my
podcast, then took their life experiences and advice and began
summarizing all of their wisdom together with mine.

The results are the nine core tenets of the *The Build a*

Bigger Life Manifesto.

This book has been written on airplanes, in coffee shops, in the wee hours of the morning before my family was awake, and was finished in the town of Sorrento, Italy, where we spent 14 glorious days in the summer of 2019 in the midst of a 25-day European adventure.

What you now hold in your hand is this guidebook in printed form. It's as much a call to my children as it is to the hundreds of thousands of people I've presented to over the years. My intense hope is that you take one, two, three, or all of the ideas in the book and apply them to your own life. And, remember as you do that you are the architect of your life experience. There is no earthly being more in control of your experiences than you. Once you accept the onus of designing and living according to that design, life gets a whole lot bigger.

Thanks for being on this path with me and all of your fellow life architects.

Here's to building a bigger life!

Tenet 1

Build on a Strong (Values) Foundation

Your parents undoubtedly raised you with a certain set of values, ways of living and of treating other people that they hoped you'd adhere to for the rest of your life. Yet something happens throughout our teens and twenties—we spend less and less time with our parents and more time with friends, co-workers, spouses, and kids. Whether you realize it or not, all of those interactions will subtly shift your personal values unless you are extremely conscious of your own core values and live them accordingly.

It's fairly obvious to state that a person living according to their highest values is someone on the right track to building a bigger life. However, just one or two compromised values can cause your life to seem very small.

I recently had the opportunity to work on a project for a company that is doing big, creative things in the financial space. On the surface, everything looked right with the opportunity. They are a fun, fast-moving group of people who love to challenge the status quo. In fact, I was so honored to be asked to participate, I turned a deaf ear to the feedback of friends and mentors. Many of them asked if I knew what I was getting myself into, and still I plowed ahead.

About a month into the project, I noticed that on the days I worked in their offices, my neck and shoulders hurt by the end of the day. My energy level was nearly zapped by the end of the week, which was not at all normal for me otherwise. Furthermore, I found myself not wanting to get up and go to work on Mondays, which is the absolute opposite of how I normally feel at the start of a week.

Throughout the contract, I kept asking my inner knower (Tenet 5), "Where is the misalignment with my values?"

Two words kept coming up: Freedom and Impact.

Freedom and flexibility are hallmark values of late Gen Xers and most Millennials.[1] Those two core values have defined my work life since 2004, and living according to them has helped me build a bigger life for me and my family in the process.

What I underestimated until this contract came about was my need for the freedom to work when and how I want and the incredible value I place on having an impact on others. While I interacted with a number of people every day, the impact that helped validate the work wasn't readily visible.

Today, I know that if I'm bidding on a project, the impact *has* to be considered right off the bat as does the ability to work on my terms in a way that supports my biggest life.

If you are someone who isn't feeling fully fulfilled in your work life, it's time to dive deep into your highest values and see what's missing. Quite often, just one minor tweak in how you work, what projects you're on, or what you're focused on will make a massive difference in how you feel at the end of the day.

Perhaps creativity is one of your highest values and you're not working on anything that allows that value to shine through. Maybe your work life doesn't require a lot of creativity but working on projects at home could really add meaning to your day. The problem may be that even those creative tasks get pushed to the back-burner for the sake of your spouse, your kids, housework, and chores.

I challenge you to find something that helps express one or more of your highest values and make that part of your daily or weekly routine. Perhaps it's being more creative, learning to play an instrument or speak a new language, putting your unique skills to a good cause, or having a conversation at work about doing more of what you love to do (and are great at).

Leveraging Your Values at Work

A week or so after one of my speaking engagements, I met a gentleman for coffee. Through our conversation, it was apparent he had a core value of connection. He was a salesman and spent his days calling on companies trying to sell them a service in a very competitive field. As a result, he was getting a lot of rude gatekeepers telling him they already had a vendor for that service. At our first meeting, I remember him saying that this business just wasn't for him, and he should probably find something else to sell. However, when pushed, he said he really believed in the product. He was just missing the closer connection with his prospects.

"What if you pursued relationships and allowed the business to come to you?" I asked.

"I wouldn't even know how to do that."

"Sure you would. You called and asked me to coffee. Just do more of that."

For the past couple of years, this gentleman has been running networking appointments on a daily basis, and his business is thriving. People see him not only as an expert networker, but as an expert in his field because he functions more like a consultant and less like a salesperson. And the best part is he goes home having fulfilled one of his highest core values (connection) almost every day. It's almost as if he doesn't have to *sell* anymore because people are buying from him and referring him business all the time.

One of my favorite podcast interviewees is Troy Wittman (Episode 44). Troy was one of the presenters at the TEDx University of Wisconsin Milwaukee event where I delivered my first TEDx talk. What most inspired me about Troy's talk was that he turned his profession as a teacher into a full-fledged calling. The students in Mr. Wittman's class don't learn the same way other kids learn. They engage their imaginations, their bodies, and their minds and have fun the entire time. Call it method teaching, interactive learning, or creative engagement; Troy calls it a passion for growth, which is one of his core values. He found that by adding elements of creativity and play in his classes, he could watch the growth in his students every semester.

Mr. Wittman's class built a time machine into the corner of his classroom. This time machine allows students to re-enact scenes from history and teach their fellow classmates based on the scripts provided by Mr. Wittman. Students enter the time machine in present day and emerge from the blinking lights and fog machine-induced haze as characters from history, complete in costumes from the time period, wigs, and sometimes terrible accents.

What happens is both hysterical and memorable. And, thanks to Mr. Wittman, these students *love* to learn. He's able to watch them grow in their knowledge, their passion for the subject matter, and their confidence as presenters of learned material.

Your Values and Relationships

A relationship expert once told me the reason couples break up is that they stop living in alignment with their own values. In effect, he said, they forget who they are or desire to be and instead are living according to the values set of the other person. Far too often, he added, the values were never defined, and the relationship was on an autopilot course for disaster.

One of the quotes that comes to the surface for me is Shakespeare's "to thine own self be true." Over the years, I've been fortunate enough to work with some very talented coaches, and the question I've heard more times than I can count is, "What is out of alignment for you?"

What I've determined that question means for me is, "what values are you not living in accordance with?"

One night, my wife was putting our boys to bed and not getting a lot of cooperation from them in the process. It had been a stressful day for her at work. After battling the boys, then passing me, fully engrossed in a television show in the living room, she went into the bedroom, closed the door, and went to bed without saying a word.

The next morning, I woke up early and wondered what would've made her react the way she did. I played back what I was doing (or not doing) in the midst of putting the boys down. One word came to the surface: helpfulness. Starting that instant, I cleaned the kitchen, emptied the dishwasher, and started a load of laundry. A dramatic shift occurs when you start to appreciate and honor other people's values.

That afternoon, after school, I gathered the family, and we all had a discussion about the values that our family runs on. The list was pretty exhaustive: helpfulness, forgiveness, humility, love, respect, responsibility, family, gratitude, hard work... I then asked my sons which of those were their top three values. For my youngest it was family, respect, and love. For my other son it was respect, responsibility, and humility.

What happened next wasn't planned, but it worked out marvelously in our favor. The two of them are often at odds, mainly because they're both insanely competitive with each other. As kids often do, they've figured out ways to mess with the other—creating conflict for conflict's sake. This usually gets them both in trouble and then creates frustration for me and my wife. After learning their top three values I asked them, "Davis, can you see that when you brag about winning, don't respect Nolan's wishes, or refuse to take responsibility for chores, it angers your brother? Nolan, can you see that Davis gets upset when you refuse to play with him and don't respect his space?"

What Are You Committed To?

This idea that we need to live in alignment and accordance with our values is not new. However, it is often forgotten. We get so wrapped up in our day-to-day existence that we don't take time to re-evaluate what is most important to us, making our lives significantly smaller over time. On Episode 133 of the Build A Bigger Life podcast, I interviewed Tracy Timm, a career counselor who graduated from Yale with a psychology degree. Tracy said something on the episode that I'll remember forever: "Many people are more committed to their circumstances than they are their values." In Tracy's work, she found that people would stay in jobs that no longer served them or their highest values because of things like time off, health care, or a generous 401k program. Yet in the midst of living their life, her new clients were experiencing health issues, depression, sleeplessness, and worry. It was in going through a values-defining exercise that they began to see the reasons for their own misery.

During the Build A Bigger Life Retreats, our participants go through a core values exercise much like the one you're about to do, and they have remarkable results. One of my favorite examples is Christine, the owner of a branding and design company based in Destin, Florida. One of Christine's core values identified at the retreat was beauty, and it shows every day in the design work and incredible branding she does for her clients. Another top value was self-worth, which often manifested itself negatively in what she was charging for her services. After some very intentional coaching, Christine raised her rates to reflect what her work was truly worth. She is living more closely in alignment with her core values today, and her thriving business is living proof.

So, your first step, the first of nine core tenets of The Build A Bigger Life Manifesto, is to identify your top five core values. You'll undoubtedly find more values that feel like a match, but we're looking for just the top five. The more closely aligned you are with those five on a daily basis, the bigger your life will become.

By narrowing down and identifying the five core elements of your values set, you can begin to build upon that foundation to create a bigger life. (It's recommended you do this solo, then compare your list with the other important people in your life, i.e. spouse, partner, kids, etc.)

As you follow the instructions below, it's best not to overthink your choices. A PhD-level researcher came back with an exhaustive list of five sets of seven values each. His life was relatively chaotic at the time, and I asked if having 35 "core" values was helping or hurting him. We quickly narrowed the list down to five that would fulfill him. I suggest you do the same.

Scan the lists below and circle the words that aptly describe your values. Try to keep the list between 10–15 on the first pass. The next step will be revealed in the following pages.

Abundance	Certainty	Depth
Acceptance	Challenge	Desire
Accomplishment	Change	Determination
Acknowledgement	Charity	Devotion
Adaptability	Clarity	Dignity
Advancement	Cleanliness	Diligence
Adventure	Clear-mindedness	Direction
Affection	Cleverness	Discipline
Alertness	Closeness	Diversity
Altruism	Conformity	Dominance
Ambition	Connection	Dreaming
Appreciation	Consciousness	Drive
Awareness	Conservation	Duty
Accountability	Consistency	Decisiveness
Accuracy	Contribution	Dependability
Achievement	Control	Determination
Balance	Conviction	Encouragement
Beauty	Cooperation	Endurance
Belonging	Courage	Energy
Benevolence	Courtesy	Enthusiasm
Bliss	Creativity	Excellence
Bravery	Curiosity	Excitement
Brilliance	Competitiveness	Experience
Candor	Contribution	Exploration
Capability	Daring	Expressiveness
Caring	Dependability	Equality

Fairness	Learning	Resolve
Faith	Logic	Resourcefulness
Family	Loyalty	Respect
Fearlessness	Leadership	Responsibility
Fitness	Legacy	Satisfaction
Flexibility	Love	Security
Focus	Making a difference	Self-control
Freedom	Mastery	Selflessness
Friendship	Mindfulness	Self-reliance
Frugality	Modesty	Self-respect
Fun	Motivation	Sensitivity
Generosity	Nature	Serenity
Grace	Openness	Service
Gratitude	Optimism	Sharing
Growth	Order	Significance
Happiness	Organization	Silence
Harmony	Patience	Silliness
Health	Passion	Simplicity
Heart	Peace	Sincerity
Honesty	Persistence	Skillfulness
Honor	Philanthropy	Solitude
Humility	Playfulness	Sophistication
Integrity	Power	Soundness
Intellect	Pragmatism	Speed
Intimacy	Precision	Spirit
Intuition	Reflection	Spirituality
Independence	Relaxation	Spontaneity
Joy	Reputation	Stability
Kindness	Resilience	
Knowledge	Resolution	

Obviously, no one can live by 20-30 core values. The very word core means the central or most important parts. The next step in Building A Bigger Life is identifying the top values that are most central to you living life on your terms.

Here's how – first, document all of the chosen values from the previous pages in the spaces below:

_____	_____	_____
_____	_____	_____
_____	_____	_____
_____	_____	_____
_____	_____	_____
_____	_____	_____
_____	_____	_____
_____	_____	_____
_____	_____	_____
_____	_____	_____

Next – isolate the top 10 from the list above:

_____	_____	_____
_____	_____	_____
_____	_____	_____
_____		

Then – from those top 10, what are the 5 that are most important to see in your life?

_____   _____   _____

_____   _____

Finally – rank those 5 values in order of importance in your life:

1. _____

2. _____

3. _____

4. _____

5. _____

What are your rules around each of your core values?

1. _____

2. _____

3. _____

4. _____

5. _____

Tenet 2

See Yourself as the Architect of Your Own Life

For the past two decades, I've kept a journal of my thoughts, my activities, my lifelong desires, and my Big Hairy Audacious Goals (BHAGs). I started doing this after hearing motivational speaker Jim Rohn say that the only thing we have to leave our children are our words and our pictures. Several times throughout the year, I'll go back and re-read what I've gone through, see what my aspirations were at the time, and compare them to the results that I've gotten. Oddly enough, what I began to notice was a direct correlation—what I'd written down months and years earlier was what I was presently experiencing. The act of journaling was itself a way of creating the blueprint for what I desired.

When I began my career in speaking, it was a goal of mine to support myself and my family completely with speaking revenue. There were entries in my journal like, "when I make $1,500 per engagement and do four per month, I'll have made it." A year and a half later, my goals had adjusted to $2,500 per engagement, and I wanted five or six per month. The first time I made over five figures a day—a goal I'd had for a couple of years—I thought I'd finally arrived. I wrote often about having travel as a part of my lifestyle, of bringing my wife or my kids with me on work trips, of speaking in destination-type cities that allowed work and family to coexist harmoniously, and of spending weeks at a time in other countries.

Through the years, there were entries about doing TED talks, creating video content that would be featured on national television, landing a book deal with a publisher, and building a media company that would educate the masses on personal and financial growth and development.

Today, I have delivered two TEDx talks. The first at the University of Wisconsin Milwaukee and the second at the London Business School. The second talk has racked up millions of views on YouTube, making it into the top 5% of the most-viewed TED talks in history. It's now a featured talk on TED.com, something that happens to only a small fraction of all talks. In 2017, my crowd-funded documentary *Broke, Busted & Disgusted* aired on CNBC for the first time, and I remember watching it with neighbors feeling awestruck at how this simple idea was now being seen by millions of people. The media company is being built at www.Mastery-OfMoney.com, the book *Mastery of Money for Students* is being used in high schools and colleges nationwide, and I'm currently working with agents on a formal book deal.

None of this I share with you to boast, brag, or to impress. My sole intent is to show you how attainable it is to manifest what you want. Especially when you view your bigger life as a relentless pursuit.

Compressing Time

A good friend of mine recently confided in me that he realized he had the power to compress the time between thinking of a goal or desire and achieving it. His goal was income-based, and he found that it was usually an 18-month process between having the goal and achieving it. However, through some mental and emotional exercises, he realized he could compress the timeframe down to six months. Now, he's able to architect and achieve his big goals within six months or less!

Try this for yourself. What is something that you've envisioned for yourself? Whether it's relationship-oriented, money-related, a business opportunity, the desire to travel, or something bigger like running a marathon, competing in a triathlon, writing a book, acting in a movie, or being location-independent. Once you've identified that big hairy audacious goal, set a timeframe for its accomplishment. The time you set for its achievement probably comes with some mental chatter about whether or not you can do it. Listen to that voice, acknowledge you heard it, then realize that voice comes from a part of your comfort zone. Its intent is to keep things in a homeostatic environment. "Lower stress, less challenge" is the comfort zone's motto.

However, what we know now through brain research is that pushing through struggle is what reshapes how our brain functions in relation to challenge,[1] whether it's an Olympic athlete pushing himself for years to beat someone by one one-thousandth of a second, a writer (who also happens to be employed full-time) getting up early every morning for six months to write her novel or screenplay, or a business owner who struggles for the first year or two but achieves the business success he set out for. Each will tell you the struggle is what made the accomplishment possible.

No Pressure, No Diamonds.

We'll revisit the timeframe you set in the coming chapters, as well as ways to compress time to bring your goal closer to existence. When you truly see yourself as the architect of your life, the visions you'll begin to have are not just visions, they'll become blueprints of what your life will ultimately be like. By leveraging the other tenets, you'll be able to make these visions possible, not in decades, not in years, but often in mere months.

What Often Gets in the Way

About three years ago, I was delivering a talk to a group of young professionals about pursuing that which fired them up. Whether it was a hobby, a business, or learning a craft or a musical instrument, my message was that they should be pursuing something they loved to do.

One attendee piped up in the middle of my talk and asked, "But what if that isn't possible?"

"Tell me more," I said.

"Well, what if financially you just can't afford to go do the things that fire you up inside?"

It is obviously not an abnormal thing for people to perceive the lack of money as the biggest obstacle to pursuing loves in their life.

"So tell me, what financially stands in the way of you pursuing your passion?"

"Well, for starters, I just leased a new car and am paying on a couch that I bought on credit..."

Her reasons for not pursuing what she most wanted (travel), largely stemmed from the fact that she was spending a great deal of her time working to pay for the stuff that she had acquired after graduation.

At the time, I didn't know it, but I coined a phrase that has become central to my podcast, many of my speaking events, and the title of this book.

"Perhaps you have it backwards," I said. "Build a bigger life, not a bigger lifestyle."

I finished writing this book on a 25-day European vacation with enough clothes for five to seven days and a small work backpack. My family traveled just as light. Trust me, you don't need all the things.

If the stuff that you're acquiring isn't getting you closer

to joy, perhaps it's time to rethink priorities from things to experiences, from stuff to simplicity.

This realization led me to start interviewing people who seemed like they had their stuff together in relation to going after their highest priorities. The interviews were pumped out on iTunes, Spotify, and Stitcher as the Build A Bigger Life podcast. And slowly but surely, an audience grew out of that podcast, and people from all over began commenting about the message and how much it inspired them.

One weekend, I received an email from someone I'd never met with the subject line: *You've changed my life.* As that is probably one of the greatest lines of clickbait ever written, I opened it. The email was from a gentleman named Tim Rose who happened to be living on the island of Oahu, pursuing his dream of being a full-time, professional musician. Tim wrote that he had heard me on the podcast talking about eliminating debt from your life and how much easier it is to live your dreams with no financial burdens. But there was one line in Tim's email that particularly stood out to me. He wrote, "Because of you, I'm living in my van."

My first thought was, "I don't remember telling anyone on a podcast to live in their vehicle!"

But Tim went on to say, *"I love my life. Every morning I wake up to the sound of the ocean and go surfing. When I'm done surfing, I shower at the beach. Then I get to do what I love to do every day—write and play music."*

Tim is a regular guy who had a father with enough sense to tell Tim *not* to go to law school and instead pursue music, which was clearly a love of his.

Here's the side story: Tim lives in a Chevy box van that he's modernized into traveling living quarters. He realized, soon after moving to Hawaii to pursue music, that paying $1,800 a month for an efficiency apartment wasn't going to get him closer to his passion. If nothing else, he was moving farther away from music and closer to working multiple jobs just to make ends meet.

That's about the time Tim realized he could trade in the truck he was driving for a box van with a similar payment. Ditch the apartment, spruce up the mobile digs, and he was in business. Literally, he operates his music business from the van (and now a rented office space where he does live music shows he broadcasts online).

In my interview with Tim, you can hear how exceptionally happy this guy is. And why wouldn't he be? He spends his mornings surfing, showers at the local beach or a friend's place, then turns his attention towards creating the one thing that matters most to him—his music. He plays around four to six shows a week in Waikiki, which makes him more than enough money to cover the living expenses he's grown accustomed to, plus the extra allows him to either blast away debt or put money away to shoot some seriously high-end music videos. And, Tim told me, he now has hope that he can one day purchase a home and support a family with his craft.

Tim Rose is absolutely building a bigger life for himself. It's only a matter of time before the guy is clearing hundreds if not thousands or tens of thousands of dollars a month from music royalties. Only a matter of time before labels are reaching out to represent him. Only a matter of time before Ed Sheeran announces his opening act… none other than Tim Rose. And only a matter of time before his music is on the soundtrack of a new movie. This dude is that good.

What started for me as a passing comment to an attendee at one of my events has grown into a bit of a movement. Tim mentions in the interview that what I said about leveraging income to its fullest extent ("Making Money Irrelevant," Tenet 7) made a huge difference in his life. But he's the one making a difference—he's living according to his highest values, is the architect of his own life, and loves what he does on a daily basis.

Tim's Build A Bigger Life podcast interview is one of my most-downloaded interviews of all time. He's exactly what you'd imagine a full-time musician-surfer living in his van on Oahu would be—totally laid back, chiseled, good-lookin', and smooth. And he's ridiculously talented to boot.

During our follow-up phone calls and Zoom chats, Tim mentioned that he wanted to do a visual album, which is a film that tells the story of his album. But the kicker was it came with about a $50,000 price tag.

As we talked through his plan to save as much as he could and borrow the rest, I asked Tim, "Why wouldn't you just ask your fans to help crowd-fund the film?" Tim's response was filled with uncertainty about whether or not his tribe would help underwrite it, feeling like it would be too much of an ask, ultimately not wanting to "bother" anyone with it.

But after a little more discussion, it was clear that this was something he was 100% committed to doing. My experience has always been if you're *that* committed, it's destined to happen. So within just a few weeks, Tim had mapped out his visual album, locked down a director and crew, and launched his crowd-funding campaign. Today, the visual album is a finished product, winning film awards, and helping to propel Tim to a new level in his music career. (I happily contributed to his campaign and now have a signed Tim Rose guitar hanging in my office!)

Whose House Would You Live In?

Let's assume that you wanted to build a house, and there were two similar lots in very similar neighborhoods. No matter which you choose, the price, size, and conveniences would conceivably all be the same. After picking one lot and beginning the building process, the builder chooses the other lot to build a spec home. In the home you are building, you get to select where the walls are placed and what all of the finishes are, including flooring, lighting, hardware—the works. Every last detail is yours to choose. The finished product perfectly fits your lifestyle, your desires, and your family.

In the builder's spec home, the builder is choosing all of the building plans and finishes according to his own preferences. While it's a reasonably comfortable home, there are aspects of it that just flat-out turn you off. Some of the rooms are too small, and your kitchen would be arranged far differently.

On the day of closing, your home and the builder's

home are both move-in ready. The builder asks if you'd be interested in living in his home instead of your own. He says he might even mark it down a bit to make it worth your while. In which house would you live?

I hope you would choose the one you were the architect of! The irony is I know dozens of people who are living a life they haven't designed for themselves. It just happens to be the one that life (the builder) gave them. The price you've paid for this house may be a bargain, but it certainly comes with a number of "amenities" you didn't choose for yourself.

Your vision for what your life should be is the blueprint to follow. Throughout this book, you'll be asked certain questions that will help you identify and clarify the bigger life that you'll be building. The key is to think of yourself as the architect. The one who makes the plans and directs the execution of the plans.

> There is **NOT ONE** earthly being who has greater control over your life than you.

Listen to Your Own Dialogue; Speak Like the Architect You Are

The idea of being the architect of your life means that the life you're living is the one you've designed for yourself.

I find that too many people take a prescribed path, but

not necessarily the one that most closely matches what they want in life. Some people believe they have no control over those sorts of things and instead ride the wave of whatever happens in hopes that one day the tide will turn in their favor. For some it does. For some it doesn't. And what separates the two, I've found, is the kind of language they use to describe their situations.

It's amazing what happens when you start to pay attention to the language other people use to describe their circumstances. Just listen over the next couple of days and count the number of times you hear, "Well I would, but I can't because my boss...," or "Yeah, we'd like to, but our kids aren't ready," or, "My uncle tried that one time and failed miserably, so we've learned from his lesson." When I started listening to the reasons people had for not living the lives they most imagined, they were largely outside of their "control." But mostly, they just weren't seeing themselves as architects, doing whatever was necessary to build the lives they fantasized about.

In Jack Canfield's best-selling book, *The Success Principles*, his #1 success principle is "Take 100% Responsibility." Canfield maintains that everything that happens in our life is ours to take responsibility for. If we don't, we are basically like ships tossed about on the open sea with no rudders, no sails, and no hopes of ever finding land. Canfield shares the equation $E + R = O$ (Event + Response = Outcome) in response to those who question whether you can take 100% responsibility for *everything*. What you have 100% responsibility for is your response to any event. No matter what the event may be, only your response can control the outcome.

In Tim Ferriss' best-selling book, *The 4-Hour Workweek*, he opens people's eyes to a new way of working, whether you are a corporate soldier or a self-employed renegade. When he published, thousands of comments on his blogs appeared from people who were taking his advice. Many comments were from people who asked their bosses if they could work from home at least a couple days a week, and it changed their lives for the better. He introduced people to the quality life of the "New Rich"—those who realized how to make their time more valuable while working less.

In effect, Ferriss suggests that people begin acting like they have a say in what happens in their lives. Don't like working every day in the office? Then why not take it upon yourself to ask if it's possible not to? That's what a life architect does. They wouldn't simply say, "Well my boss wouldn't allow it," without at least *asking*! Complaining about the current situation does nothing but add to the negativity associated with it. Doing and/or saying something is the architect's way.

To continuously see yourself as the architect of your life, it's necessary to do a couple of things:

1. Isolate and eliminate language that you use to describe situations "out of your control."

2. Realize that everything you do in life is a choice. You are either choosing it, or you are changing it.

Let's start with #1. The language that you use on a regular basis is the product of your subconscious mind, by and large. This part of you was formed at a very young age, absorbed lots of messages along the way, and began living according to those messages whether they served you or not. Many environmental factors help shape who you are and the language you use, and most people are not in control of this.

Your subconscious mind comes up with reasons you can't or shouldn't do something bold, brave, and new on a continual basis. It's part of your natural defense mechanism to keep the status quo, to avoid pain, and to protect that which you believe to be true (at the time).

Your subconscious mind exists to do two things well—protect the mind and body, and to answer complex questions efficiently. It does both simultaneously and sometimes to the detriment of us living bigger lives.

As an example, "why" questions are some of the worst to ask your subconscious mind (particularly if you're not used to seeing yourself as the architect).

Ask yourself:

Why haven't I gotten a raise (or a bigger raise) lately?

Why can't I find a man/woman to spend the rest of my life with?

Why does this always happen to me?

Why would they call and tell me this on a Monday?

Why can't I get my finances under control?

The answers to these questions (that many people are asking themselves on a daily basis) are usually negative because your subconscious looks for a way to efficiently answer complex questions. And they're not only negative, but they protect the mind and body, keeping you from accomplishing what it is you want in life because, ultimately, it's never your responsibility.

The answers:

> Because my boss wouldn't know talent if it bit him in the ass.
>
> Because all men are pigs, because most women are stuck on themselves.
>
> Because you were born under a bad sign, and it's not your fault.
>
> Because last week was a good week, so you're destined to have a bad one.
>
> Because your parents screwed up your money programming so... again, not your fault.

Step one in seeing yourself as the architect is realizing that the language you've been using to describe situations outside of your control keeps the situations out of your control. You're consciously or subconsciously making a choice *not* to be the architect. The thoughts you think and language you use are literally creating an out-of-control situation.

Keep this in mind:

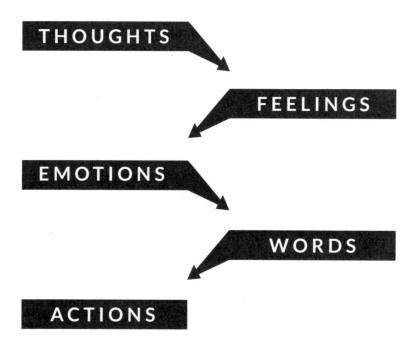

If your thoughts are "this isn't fair," they more than likely generate a feeling of helplessness. That feeling will likely generate an emotion of sadness or depression. The words used when you're sad or depressed are generally limiting, and the actions that correspond could include binge-watching Netflix and eating ice cream all weekend. None of which change the situation!

The opposite thought would be asking yourself, "What can I learn from this?" which might make you feel down, but definitely not out. The emotion that comes from this is hope, which generates hopeful words and likely positive action.

Step two in seeing yourself as the architect is realizing that everything you do is a choice.

You didn't get a bigger raise because you chose not to challenge the given raise, or you didn't perform at an excellent level.

You don't have someone in your life because you're choosing to not let people in.

You have bad things happen in your life because you're attracting them with your attitude.

You were called on a Monday and you *chose* to give that call meaning or not.

Your finances are a result of choices you've made, plain and simple. Choose to spend less and save more.

You are either choosing the life you're living, or you're changing it. There are no other options.

Once you realize there is a cause and effect for everything in your life, you'll begin to see yourself as the architect and start making decisions to build a bigger life. One of my favorite quotes is, *"Your life is perfectly engineered to get the results you're getting."* Let's re-engineer your life to get the life you want!

Tenet 3

Holding a Bigger Vision

Diego Corzo was fourteen years old when he first found out that he was an undocumented immigrant living in the United States. He was signing up for a school soccer team, and when he was asked for his Social Security number, his mother informed him he didn't have one.

At the time, there wasn't a "dreamer" category for people like Diego. They were simply undocumented. However, Diego had (and has always had) huge aspirations. He was not going to be deterred by not having this paperwork.

He worked hard throughout school, graduating at nearly the top of his high school class. He was accepted to Florida State University but realized in the process that without a Social Security number, he wouldn't be able to borrow student loans to go to school. His parents, also undocumented, wouldn't be able to co-sign on anything, nor had they been able to save the kind of money it took to attend FSU.

If Diego was going to make it through college, he was going to have to do it on his own.

Diego's vision was probably highly unrealistic to most people. He had visions of graduating from college debt-free, of building a real estate portfolio someday, and eventually establishing a company. He even had the audacity to think about what financial freedom would look like before he turned 30!

After applying for every scholarship he could find (and winning several), he was denied the awards given his citizenship status. Diego ultimately found himself facing a shortfall on tuition and having to find a way to cover it.

When we have a big vision, it is often the catalyst for new ideas, introductions to the right people, and finding circumstances that open new doors. For Diego, the vision of graduating from college debt-free and building businesses led him to a friend named Pascal Wagner. Pascal and Diego realized they had similar passions when it came to business, and they both had skills building websites. So the two formed an LLC, opened a business account in the LLC's name, and began selling websites to companies in and around the FSU area.

The business thrived during their college years, making them both a steady income that allowed them to pay for tuition in cash every time the bill came due. Diego ended up graduating debt-free, perpetually thinking about how to accomplish his big vision.

While in school, Diego had interned at General Motors,

and they saw great promise in this firebrand. He was intense and hardworking, while being affable and fun to be around. They offered him a job upon graduation at their plant in Austin, Texas.

It was around this time that President Obama introduced an executive order, called The Dreamer Act, giving minors of undocumented individuals certain privileges similar to citizens of the U.S.

What happened next would be a challenge Diego was used to dealing with. The HR department at General Motors informed him that because he was undocumented, he wouldn't be able to be hired at GM until the Dreamer Act was passed by Congress. Again, undeterred by circumstance and driven by his vision, Diego reached out to the gentleman who had offered him the job and asked if he could hire his LLC as a contractor for the position until the paperwork had been sorted out. They agreed, and Diego was now working for a Fortune 100 company.

However, Diego's challenges were not over. Without the appropriate paperwork, Diego wasn't able to get his driver's license and had been relying on rides from friends like Pascal throughout college. Now that he was accepting a professional position several states away, he was facing the issue of getting to work every day without wheels of his own.

He ultimately did what any life architect with a big vision would do—he stepped up to the challenge. In the Texas heat, Diego rode a bike to and from work every day for six months.

The Dreamer Act was signed and made law on

December 8, 2010, allowing Diego to become a full-time employee of GM and finally obtain a driver's license.

Diego excelled at GM, moving up through the ranks easily, yet still part of his vision was eluding him. He was a student of real estate investing and wanted to begin building the empire that would ultimately allow him to create financial freedom. Diego began the courses necessary to get his real estate license and put himself under the guidance of some of the top agents in Austin. Within months, he was working with buyers at nights and on weekends, keeping his day job at GM.

He began scoping out properties that would be great investments, and soon he had secured funding from friends and relatives to purchase some of them himself. With each of the properties he purchased, he leveraged something called "house hacking," whereby the landlord fills each of the rooms of the house with a tenant who may or may not know each other. By doing so, Diego's profits per property soared.

With his real estate career taking off and his rental properties bringing in consistent income after just two short years of working at GM, Diego approached his manager to let him know he'd be leaving to pursue real estate full-time.

Diego's vision of becoming financially free is well on its way. At 28 years old, Diego owns nearly 20 units, and his monthly passive income covers 75% of his expenses. By the time he's 30, Diego will have achieved his version of the American dream.

In 2019, Diego was asked to tell his story from a TEDx stage at a college in Texas. You can hear Diego tell his story in his own words by searching "Diego Corzo TEDx" on

YouTube. Diego achieved what most people never will by the time he was 28, and today his vision continues to expand. You can listen to Diego on podcast episodes 27 and 132 to learn from this life architect.

The Bigger the Vision, the Better

American architect Daniel Burnham (one of the lead architects in the city planning of notable places like Chicago and downtown Washington, D.C.) once said, "Make no little plans. They have no magic to stir man's blood. Make big plans; aim high in hope and work."

In building a bigger life, it's your vision that is constantly drawing you forward toward the goals that you deem most important. Just a couple of years ago, I wrote down a vision of an extended family vacation to Europe, one where the entire family would get to experience what it's like to live locally for a period of time. I romanticized what it would be like to live in a villa on the Amalfi Coast of Italy for a month or more, exploring the coast and enjoying the food while I wrote in the morning and evening hours. I envisioned a house that was big enough for all of us, ideally with access to a pool, and the kinds of experiences my kids would remember forever.

As I write this, my wife and kids are playing board games on the patio of a villa high in the hills of Sorrento, Italy. I'm on a lounge chair near our private pool under the shade of an umbrella, enjoying Italian coffee and the most amazing view of the Italian coastline you can imagine. You can read about the experience and see the photos at www.buildabiggerlife.com/Sorrento.

While the vision took some time to materialize, had I never had the bigger vision, I never would've gotten to experience this in real life. What is your bigger vision? Is it in front of you on a daily basis? Have you put it away somewhere and forgotten all about it? You do have one, right?!

What I've found in working with individuals who want more out of life is that they're stuck in small thinking. It's not that they intentionally made "little plans," but instead they've forgotten that the bigger visions are necessary to build a bigger life. In many cases, they've either not given themselves permission to think bigger, or the thought of possibly not achieving the big vision has stopped them in their tracks.

My mentor, Jack Canfield, shared with me two principles that allow me to have bigger visions without feeling like I'm setting myself up to fail. First, he suggested becoming an inverse paranoid. While a paranoid person believes that the world and everyone in it is against them, an inverse paranoid believes that the world and everyone in it is conspiring on their behalf. Being an inverse paranoid has me waking up every day wondering what kind of wonderful events might happen that day. And no matter the event, if they're all done on my behalf, it's easier to see the positive in all of them.

Secondly, Jack suggested that no matter the goal, I should have *high intention* and *low attachment*. My intentions are always to accomplish my bigger visions, but if they should not happen exactly as I saw them, the attachment to the vision should not be so much as to feel let down. If the intentions are high and the attachment is low, no matter what happens as you progress toward the bigger vision, it can always be considered forward progress, if not a win. When we crowd-funded the documentary *Broke, Busted & Disgusted*, lots of people asked what would happen if we didn't meet our funding goal. My gut response was, "It's my every intention *to* meet the funding goal." And the response I got often was, "Yeah, but what if you don't?"

High intention means you put absolutely zero energy into the "what if it doesn't happen" scenario. While we made (and exceeded) our funding goal, had it not happened, I would not have felt depressed or struck down because my attachment to *that particular outcome* was low. I knew our documentary would be made. This was just one way to do it, and my intention was very high for it to happen.

My vision for the documentary was for it to be seen by millions of people, not just to be made. So after the film was finished, we began the search for a media partner that would pick up the film and air it nationally. It was about nine months later that CNBC made an offer for the film and aired it half a dozen times throughout 2017. I'll explain how I used Tenet 6 (Leverage the P.O.W.E.R. of Connections) to land CNBC, but suffice it to say, if my big vision wasn't in place, it never would've happened.

What Is Your Bigger Vision?

This is the exercise that should get your heart pumping

with excitement. When you think about what it's like to build a bigger life, what *exactly* does that bigger life look like? To be clear, it's not necessarily about stuff, though for some it may be a bigger house or a vacation home somewhere. But deep down, what is it you'd like to experience on a daily basis? How could you have more of that, and what would your life look like if you did?

Keep in mind that a bigger life may mean doing less. Like, a lot less. In episode 144 of the Build a Bigger Life podcast, Zeona McIntyre, a woman who has built a business teaching others how to leverage Airbnb to create freedom, challenged me on the notion of "bigger." Her reaction to my question, "What does it mean to build a bigger life?" has caused me to reframe my question to others who may seek less, not more. One of the attendees at the Build a Bigger Life retreat had a similar situation. His bigger vision was to scale back his business which had gotten more and more stressful over the years. It meant less income, but a whole lot more peace. Whether your bigger vision is truly *bigger*, or *smaller*, spend time writing exactly what you'd like to experience in the coming year.

This is not a "quick and dirty" exercise. It's a Friday night with a bottle of creative juice or a full-on weekend day at a coffee shop, a bookstore, or wherever you go to get creative. Get specific, as well, for the more specific your vision, the easier it is to determine what you'll need to get it.

Tenet 4

Asking Bigger Questions

With Tenet 2, you discovered the power of being the architect of your own life. Next, you learned the story of Diego Corzo and what having a bigger vision for your life does to keep you motivated and on the right path. Ultimately, the plan you make for your life is either pulling you toward what you want or keeping you in neutral. In this chapter, you'll come to understand how to unlock the power of your subconscious by asking bigger questions.

In Peter Senge's book, *The 5th Discipline*, he writes about the vision we have for our lives. The vision exists out in the distance, always pulling us closer to what we truly want in life. The vision has a pulling effect, almost as if there is a rubber band stretched around us and it simultaneously. At the same time, a metal stake pierces the ground behind us, the opposite direction from our vision. The stake represents our perceived reality. The reason many people haven't achieved what they want is because their perceived reality says they're too young, too old, not smart enough, don't have enough money, time, talent, etc. So they succumb to their perceived reality.

Asking bigger questions is ultimately about turning the inner critic (that part of you that only pays attention to the perceived reality and not to the vision) into an inner coach. The inner coach is a master question-asker who constantly strives to achieve the vision. The greatest coaches I've ever had are all masterful questioners.

As your inner coach begins taking over and asking great questions, the questions you begin asking yourself will only get bigger and bigger over time. Here's why:

We've already covered the role of the subconscious mind in Tenet 2: See Yourself as the Architect of Your Own Life, but as a refresher, the subconscious mind exists to preserve the mind and body and to answer complex questions efficiently. Most questions that we're asking on a daily basis are fairly small and not at all life-changing. Your subconscious mind is capable of answering significantly difficult questions and is able to come up with complex solutions while you sleep, but most people just don't engage their brains that way. It's like driving a Lamborghini and keeping it right around 10 mph. Some people keep it parked in a storage garage down the street.

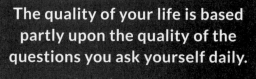

> The quality of your life is based partly upon the quality of the questions you ask yourself daily.
> – Dr. John DeMartini

If you aspire to greater success, fulfillment, accomplishment, health, better relationships, etc. in your life, part of the Build a Bigger Life equation lies in the questions you're asking yourself. Many people find themselves stuck in their current situation, but they're asking the wrong questions to break through to the next level.

Commonly asked questions include:

What else could go wrong?

What if my mother was right?

What is the worst thing that's likely to happen?

What could go wrong next?

What did I do to deserve this?

Why does this always happen to me?

Why can't I catch a break?

Why today, of all days?

Why can't anyone understand me?

Why am I being punished?

How can no one else see this needs to be done?

How come I'm always to blame?

How did this go sideways?

How am I supposed to get all this done?

How about a little help?

For some, these questions might not be pointed at your life as a whole, but at the circumstances of a single day. According to *TechCrunch*, Americans watch over five hours of TV per day.[1] It's fairly clear that the question on most of America's mind is, "What's on TV tonight?"

But ask anyone who's accomplished "a great deal" by society's standards, and they'll tell you that they watch very little television. A past mentor of mine once told me that TV and radio are simply chewing gum for the mind. They are things we engage in just to while away the time and keep our minds from focusing on bigger visions or asking bigger questions.

In episode 40 of the Build a Bigger Life podcast, I discussed the idea that our lives are perfectly engineered to get the results we're getting. If you're currently making $50,000 a year, and you ask yourself what it would take to make $60,000, you'd no doubt have an answer. Your subconscious mind would crank away, and a $60k-per-year idea would hit you in a dream or while you were driving.

Ask yourself what it would take to make $500,000 a year or $5,000,000, and your mind would crank on that a bit longer, but eventually come up with ideas just as though you'd asked it for an extra $10k. Moreover, if you asked yourself over and over what it would take to make $500k or $5M, eventually your mind would begin cranking out ideas left and right. Even further, you'd start attracting people into your life who were either making that kind of money or knew how to and were asking the same questions.

Is it possible you've been asking yourself smaller questions than you believe your mind can handle?

Holding a bigger vision (Tenet 3) will change the size of the questions you're asking. What if you were asking yourself questions about the ideal partner? The ideal marriage? The ideal business? The ideal vacation? The ideal way to raise your children? The ideal fitness plan? The ideal version of yourself and how to achieve it? The ideal life, bigger and better than you could ever imagine?

What if you adjusted your schedule so that one night a week you turned off the television and focused on answering these questions?

What *could* change in your life that would make a massive impact?

What if you answered these questions among your friends or your family?

What might happen if everyone around you knew the answers to some of the biggest questions you've been asking yourself (and them)?

One of the greatest examples of people asking bigger questions is Peter Diamandis. In his book, *Bold*, Peter talks about how his companies XPrize, Health Longevity Institute, and Planetary Resources came about. It was all about asking the question, "How would we improve this business model, this industry, or this world ten times over?" Imagine the power of asking a 10x question… that's how you go from 50k a year to 500k to 5M a year.

If you haven't heard of Peter Diamandis, look him up. He made a bold offer several years ago that he'd give $10M to the person who could build a commercial manned spacecraft that could do two launches into orbit within a certain amount of time.

He had no money to back up the claim at the time, but he began asking which companies would be interested in sponsoring a contest like this and eventually found his backer in the Ansari family. His Xprizes now fan out over multiple industries and have many sponsors and financial backers. By the way, the winner of the original Ansari Xprize sold their design to Richard Branson, who is now building Virgin Galactic using their vehicle as the prototype. All from asking bigger questions.

The other questions Peter asked involved his health and longevity. With DNA decoding getting cheaper and cheaper, Diamandis started asking, "What would it take for 100 to be the new 60?" His answers led him and his mastermind partners down a road that eventually created Health Longevity Institute that is working on keeping people healthy and thriving longer. It's bio-hacking at its finest, and they will be among the forerunners of this kind of science. All from asking bigger questions.

And finally, probably the biggest question of all came from *Star Trek* and the idea that there are things that will one day be built in space. What if you didn't have to transport stuff from Earth (and stuff is a very technical term), but instead were able to mine the building resources you needed from asteroids and other planets? That's crazy talk, right? Yet part of the challenge with the International Space Station is that the equipment and parts they need to do repairs have to be transported up with astronauts who are being blasted into space. The cost is extremely high, particularly when you figure in the added weight of parts and supplies per launch. Peter and his big question-askers began wondering, "What if you didn't have to transport materials, but obtain them from space and use 3-D printers to build the parts right there in the space station?" It sounds like science fiction, but it's very real and currently happening. All from asking bigger questions.

So you may be thinking, "Okay, what do I do with this?" And my answer is, "Challenge your current thinking and question-asking with bigger, more profound questions." Ask the 10x question in terms of your health, and your search may find people like The Iron Cowboy, who ran 50 IronMan Triathlons in 50 days in 50 states. Tell me that wasn't the product of a big question.

Ask yourself the 10x question as it applies to your income, and you'll no doubt find the stories of people who had an inspired idea and turned it into a billion-dollar website in 24 months.

And if you aren't the biggest question-asker in your family, turn this advice on your parents or your children. My kids ask big questions and have big visions, and one day, there is no doubt they'll achieve a version of their own answers. One night, my son asked, "What does it take to get drafted to the NBA from high school?" The answer was an exhaustive search on all of the people who were drafted in high school and what it took to get there. It created quite a discussion, and a determined 11-year-old trying to dunk on our lowered basketball hoop.

Now, will this (probably) average-sized kid make it to the NBA? It's not statistically likely. But the questions he's asking himself will take him down a path far different from the one he would've traveled by asking, "Why couldn't I have been born to taller parents?"

Remember, the role that the subconscious mind plays is to preserve and protect the body as well as to answer complex questions. So to fire up that incredible supercomputer in the back of your noggin, consider asking yourself the following questions when confronted with a challenging situation:

What can I learn from this?

What is one way all parties could benefit in this situation?

What is going right?

What skills should I brush up on to make this easier?

Why am I in a perfect place right now to have this experience?

Why is now the right time?

Why should I take this bold step forward?

Why are they confident in my abilities?

How has life prepared me for this moment?

How will I achieve 10x my current results?

How can I grow from this setback?

How can I get all of this completed on time?

How might I ask for help and get it?

There are a myriad of questions written into the Build A Bigger Life Blueprint available from buildabiggerlife.com. Download the PDF and take yourself through the blueprint that has changed things dramatically for me and my family. These are just some of the questions I've asked along my journey to creating a bigger life:

If happiness was the national currency, what kind of work would make me rich?

If the average human life span was 40 years, how would I live my life differently?

What one thing have I not done that I really want to do?

What makes me, me?

At what time in my recent past have I felt the most passionate and alive?

What would I do differently if I knew nobody would judge me?

What am I pretending not to know?

What are my values, and how could I be truer
to them?

What did I learn today?

If I wasn't scared, what would I do?

What do I want my life to be like in 5 years?

What's the one most important thing to get done
today/this week/this month?

How would my role models act and carry themselves?

What do I absolutely love in life?

What are my greatest accomplishments in life so far?

If my life had absolutely no limits, and I could have it all
and do whatever I wanted, what would I choose to have,
and what would I choose to do?

What are the top five things I cherish in my life?

What would I regret not doing?

If a doctor gave me one year to live, what would I
try to accomplish?

What does success mean to me?

How could I describe myself in five words?

What am I doing to pursue my dreams right now?

If I left my current life in order to pursue my dreams,
what would I lose?

How would I describe the next five years of my life
in a sentence?

Keep in mind that the questions you ask may take time
to answer. Your subconscious is working whether you're
awake or asleep. One suggestion is to pepper your subconscious with a few of these questions and let it chew on them
overnight or while you're doing something mindless like
cleaning the house or exercising. What I've found most often
is that the answers come when I least expect them.

While asking bigger questions is definitely something
you can do by yourself, by bringing in significant others,
mastermind partners, and friends, the answers that are created
may be ten times as powerful as your answers alone.

Just know, in your core, that the answers came from a
part of you that is engineered to answer complex questions
efficiently!

Tenet 5

Trusting the Inner Knower

By now, you're in tune with living according to your values foundation, you're seeing yourself as the architect of your own life, holding a bigger vision, and asking bigger questions. The next step is to trust the "inner knower."

I was introduced to the idea of an inner knower by my friend, mastermind partner, and spiritual Sherpa, Mitch Matthews. Mitch pioneered a program called The Big Dream Gathering, which brings together people from all walks of life to share their "big dreams" and help each other figure out how to achieve them. He's a successful author, podcaster, speaker, and all-around insanely good human.

During a particularly challenging time in my life and business, I called Mitch on the way to my office to get some advice. I had started a mortgage brokerage, we had just had our third child, and I was still building my speaking business whenever I had time. The challenges I faced were needing a greater cash flow, managing some employee issues, and feeling like I didn't have enough time to get everything done. Mitch asked me a number of really big, powerful questions that he suggested I meditate on a while.

One of the most meaningful questions he asked was, "Where are you closest to money?" The question was really about how to solve my cash flow challenges, but it was engineered so that my mind was focused on where the easiest, fastest, and closest opportunities were.

Mitch's suggestion was to pose the question, then get really quiet and listen. My immediate response was, *"What am I listening for?"*

"You'll know," he said. "Just trust it."

When I got to my office, I wrote "Where am I closest to money?" on a sheet of paper in front of me, sat back in my chair, and closed my eyes. I listened for the answer.

It took all of three minutes to calm my mind with some deep breaths, the whole time questioning the validity of his process. Then a name popped into my head, someone I'd known from college who was now working at a local community college in the student activities office. I wrote her name down on the sheet of paper and closed my eyes again.

The next name came seemingly out of nowhere. It was a guy I had networked with three weeks earlier, someone that didn't strike me as holding the key to immediate money, but again, trusting the advice of my friend, I wrote his name down on the sheet.

What happened next validated everything Mitch had

told me. I looked up the number to my friend from college and called her immediately.

"Hey, Erin. It's Adam. I got a nudge to call you today just to see what's happening with you."

Then she said the magic words that I'm certain you've heard before.

"Adam, *I was just thinking about you.* That's so weird that you called." Erin went on to tell me that she just took a new role and was looking for a speaker for an event at the end of the month. I was the first person on her shortlist, but in the wake of her new responsibilities, she hadn't had a chance to reach out yet.

We solidified the details over the phone. In that moment, I had secured enough cash flow to get me through the challenge. The entire call lasted about 25 minutes.

Curious about whether or not I could go two for two, I called the second name on my list and happened to get him on the phone.

"Hey, Kevin. It's Adam. I'm following up to see if there's anything I can do to help. Call me crazy, but I had a nudge to call you today."

Kevin was pleasantly surprised to get my call, and while he didn't have any pressing need to pay me for my services, he mentioned passing my name along to a friend of his who was planning a company retreat. "It wouldn't surprise me if he reaches out to you soon."

I asked if he minded if I reached out to his friend. *"The way these events go,"* I said, *"it's generally the person they've spoken to most recently who gets the business."*

Kevin gave me his friend's name and number. We agreed to stay in touch, and I committed to letting him know the outcome of my call. By noon, I had received a call back from Kevin's contact inquiring about my speaking fees and the programs I offered.

Nothing closed immediately with the second call, but the friend ended up referring me to a fellow business owner in his networking group who hired me about two months later.

If you're a naturally skeptical person, you could easily wave this off as being purely coincidental. To be perfectly candid, I would've had the exact same reaction had it not physically happened to me, not once, but over and over and over again in the last ten years.

You could call the inner knower just about anything you like: intuition, a higher power, God, the collective conscious, your subconscious, the divine, your spirit guides. Whatever you personally call the voice that comes to you in moments like this, are you asking it bigger questions and then trusting in the answers?

Which Voice is Louder?

There are actually two voices that I (and many other people I've interviewed) hear. One is the inner knower. It's the wise, all-knowing voice that seems to have a connection to information your rational mind doesn't. To hear it, you must be able to sit very quietly and listen for it.

Then, there is the voice of the inner critic. The inner critic is louder than the inner knower. I've heard it described as "the machine" because it tends to operate on auto-pilot. It's not programmed so much as it has materialized over time, and generally has a very negative tone to it. The machine is a combination of your ego, your protective mechanisms, and your perspective on the world. It can't be trusted to give you the information that the inner knower can.

The greatest challenge you will likely have (though will easily overcome) is trusting the inner knower and challenging the machine. To do this, it's necessary to hear what the machine has to say, and then to challenge it by asking, "If I listen to that voice, where will it keep me stuck?" Because the machine is the combination of things mentioned above, it is generally coming from a place that is protective of the status quo. Its job is to help put meaning on things that justify your current place in life.

It's the inner knower that will actually tell you the truth according to your core values and your vision.

In my experience, getting in touch with my inner knower requires a few minutes of calm and quiet. Because I'm easily distracted by bright, shiny objects, the best way for me to hear the answers to the questions I'm asking myself is to be in a dark room with my eyes closed, listening to alpha wave music, and with a set of questions. I've been working consciously on hearing it in daily life as well, though it is a very gradual process.

I've recorded a special guided meditation for this book that will help you get quiet and hear the inner knower. It's available for download at www.buildabiggerlife.com/recordings.

If you're not someone who has a meditation practice, I'm going to be the millionth person to tell you why it's crucial. Our lives have become more and more fast-paced, and we're constantly bombarded by images of what we "should" be doing. Whether it's an Instagram story, a Facebook feed, a television commercial, or advice from the latest guru on a morning talk show. Consider that some of the most valuable companies in the world today—Facebook, Apple, Netflix, and Google—are all designed to distract you.

However, only you know deep down what you most want in life. Without adopting some form of meditation, you're likely to succumb to the numbing power of what society deems important. Because that message is loud, it's persistent, and it chokes out individuality as if it was sent here to do so. What the world needs is the most authentic, intentional, and alive you there is.

In my opinion, the tenets listed and the exercises outlined in this book will help you get there, but meditation will *guarantee* that you get there. When you calm the choppy waters of your mind and can see all the way down to the bottom, that's when your life gets bigger. The inner knower lives in there somewhere and is just waiting for you to listen intently.

Tenet 6

Leveraging the P.O.W.E.R. of Connection

My grandfather ran for the governor's seat in the state of Iowa in 1973. He was a lightning rod candidate as his campaign platform was to legalize marijuana, prostitution, and gambling. His intent was to place a heavy tax on all of them and use the money to fund social service programs. You could say he was a bit ahead of his time. So much ahead that he lost in the primaries to a centrist Democrat who ended up losing the gubernatorial race to Robert Ray, a Republican and one of the most beloved governors the state of Iowa has ever had.

My grandpa ran a very grassroots operation, covering the state in a vehicle with three or four cronies, sleeping on couches and in cheap motels. He was completely opposed to taking money from special interest groups. He talked about getting rid of money in politics until the day he died.

In running a grassroots campaign, my grandpa relied on the kindness, generosity, and hard work of other people. He didn't have much in the way of resources to pay them, but what he did have were contacts and connections, a way of making people feel important, and an insane ability to remember names.

When my cousins and I were younger, our grandpa would take us with him around town, running errands and stopping at the houses of friends of his who were ill or couldn't get out of their homes. We always made a stop at Dahl's grocery store, one of his favorite haunts, typically because he wanted to pick up some Breyer's Ice Cream for "us" (but really for him). While there, he'd get stopped in the aisles over and over again by people who knew him. And amazingly, he would know every single person's name whether he'd just seen them yesterday or a decade ago.

I remember asking him repeatedly, "How do you know that person?" And he would say he knew them from the campaign days or once helped that person find a job when they were out of work. For those he hadn't seen in a decade, we always marveled at how he remembered their names.

He bent down and looked me in my eyes, his firm hand on my shoulder. "Remember this," he told me, "the sweetest sound in the world to another person is their own name."

That little tidbit stuck with me and resurfaced when I read *How to Win Friends & Influence People* by Dale Carnegie. Every tip and tactic my grandpa had passed to me was in this book. To this day, it is still the second best-selling book of all time next to the Bible, and one I wholeheartedly recommend people read.

As I watched my grandpa go through life calling people by name and figuring out ways to help them achieve their goals, I realized he was just leveraging the power of his connections. And it seemed to me the more he leveraged this power, the more the power grew.

I took the model I learned from him, put structure and a framework behind it, and started using it in my own life, first when I graduated from college and then as I ventured into entrepreneurship.

Where Are You Taking the Conversation?

I did some research related to how conversations are generally started. What I found is that people usually ask five questions when sparking a new, casual conversation:

What's your name?

Where are you from?

What do you do?

How long have you done it?

What do you do for fun?

Then, the conversation usually turns a bit awkward, and we venture into three other potential categories:

The weather (Can you believe this rain? Cold? Heat?)

Sports (Are you watching the finals this weekend?)

Work (So what exactly do you do at your job?)

Now, here's the problem. Once I know the answers to the first five questions, there's not much I can help you with in the grand scheme of building our relationship. So I stopped asking the same old five questions and three categories of chatter. Instead I started asking people things like:

What are you passionate about?

What big or small projects are you personally working on right now?

What's something you'd love to do but haven't yet done?

If you had a million dollars tomorrow, what would you do to give your life meaning?

The answers I received were from people who wanted to write a book or a screenplay, wanted to dig wells in Africa, wanted to climb Mount Kilimanjaro, wanted to skydive, wanted to backpack across Australia… They were BIGGER LIFE things that were closer than these people realized. Now I was able to leverage the power of my connections.

To understand what I mean, it might help to know that while my grandpa had lots of brushes with greatness and could've been a very wealthy man, he instead focused on a different kind of wealth measured in social capital.

Social capital is something all of us have. It's worth more than commodities or equities and certainly worth more than currency. Social capital is the dormant value of our connections with friends, family, and colleagues. Value that can be easily traded or exchanged. And my grandpa had a lot of it.

But here's the kicker: Even when you trade or exchange social capital, its value grows. And the greater your social capital, the faster and easier it is to build a bigger life. As Zig Ziglar famously put it, "If you help enough other people get what they want, you can't help but get what you want."

The framework I put around my grandpa's philosophy is called P.O.W.E.R., an acronym that stands for:

Promoting Opportunities While Establishing Relationships

I realized that I connected with people more when I asked the questions as listed above. I was getting answers that would allow me to promote opportunities to them while establishing our relationship (P.O.W.E.R.). Without those questions, I had no way of helping other people get closer to what they wanted.

My logic behind this was based primarily on Google.

If you were going to write a paper today, the first place you'd go to do your research would be Google. When you type in your search term on Google, you're more than likely going to get millions of hits, and they'll show up in milliseconds. The explanation of this lies in the countless billions of connected computers within the Internet, all posting information related to whatever your search was. In effect, the more connected the computers are, the faster and more relevant the information that comes back to you.

Similarly, in your brain, there are millions of neural pathways allowing impulses to travel and transfer information.

The more interconnected the neural pathways, the faster the impulses travel, and the easier it is to recall information.

So if it's true with computers, and it's true with your brain, wouldn't it also be true that the more interconnected we are personally and socially, the faster and easier we can get to what we want? (i.e., to build a bigger life in less time than you could possibly imagine)

The challenge in this experiment of mine was getting people to realize that just by sharing their bigger life goals with other people in their network, they were far more likely to achieve what they ultimately wanted in the short and long term.

The Network of Connections

I wanted to put this theory to the test and came up with the "network of connections" exercise that I've done at hundreds of events across the country. I can think of only two instances where it didn't produce amazing results, and both were because the audience wasn't high on the participation scale.

My idea was that if I asked a group of people what their dream job was, or to tell me about a project they were working on that could use some assistance, or even what they wanted to do or experience in life, that someone in the audience would have contacts or experience that would be beneficial to that person. If we all approached the exercise as though it was a challenge to see how many people we could get to their bigger vision, we'd all win. To make the exercise more visual, I started carrying a ball of yarn with me to events and would "string together" everyone who made a connection in the fifteen minutes of sharing. Then, and purely for the purpose of showing off, I'd call everyone by name just to illustrate how easy it is to remember names if you're actually paying attention.

The first event at which I tried this confirmed my hypothesis that in every audience, there are people who can help you achieve your bigger life vision. At the introductory "network of connections" attempt, the conference audience was significantly smaller than I had hoped due to a snowstorm keeping over half of the attendees stranded in airports or at home. However, I was determined to find out whether this exercise would work no matter the size of the room. So with 35 to 40 people in the room, I began by asking this group of college students and recent graduates if any of them had their dream job or dream internship in mind.

The first young man to raise his hand said he wanted to work as an accountant for an NHL team. This was a far more specific and higher-echelon job than I was hoping for on the first round, but I gave it a shot, "Does anyone here have contacts within the NHL?"

Immediately, another young man in the back of the room raised his hand and said, "My best friend's grandpa owns the Boston Bruins." With that, the first volunteer nearly jumped out of his skin. "Would you be willing to make an introduction, if nothing else than to give him a contact name, email, or phone number?" I asked.

"Of course," the first young man said.

I then asked the guy with the NHL contact what his

dream job or internship would be.

His answer was, "Doing Teach For America." I turned to the audience and asked, "Does anyone have any contacts within Teach For America?"

A young lady in the front of the room raised her hand and said, "The past president of our chapter is a recruitment director for Teach For America." Immediately, we connected the two of them with string and kept going.

At this point, I was ecstatic that my theory was playing out in real life, especially with such a small group of people.

The young lady mentioned that she'd like to try her hand at modeling and another young woman knew the owner of a talent agency that had offices in Denver and Chicago. The second young woman said she would love to work for a Big Four accounting firm and be based in Atlanta. So, naturally, one of the attendees had a former fraternity brother who was working in the Atlanta office for Ernst & Young and would be a great contact.

It went just like this for the next 20 minutes, and we connected 15 people within ONE DEGREE of their dream job. At the end of the exercise, I asked the group what most surprised them about what had just happened, and their overwhelming response was, *"I didn't realize how close I could be to what I really want in life!"*

As I previously said, I've done this exercise hundreds of times all across the country, and the results (when the audience is willing to open themselves up) is always the same. Those who participate end up finding a contact who can help them get closer to what they've always wanted.

While the first exercise was about dream jobs and internships, the "network of connections exercise" has helped people dig wells in Africa, climb Mt. Kilimanjaro, write books, book TED talks, close sales deals, travel internationally, and even land acting gigs in Hollywood. What I realized in all of these examples is that people have a high degree of interest in helping other people. Especially when it's helping them achieve one of their highest life ambitions.

Your bigger life vision, no matter what it is, is likely closer than you could possibly imagine, and someone in your network of contacts has a shortcut, a special hookup, an elusive contact, the secret handshake, or the private email that you need to achieve that thing you desire.

Your P.O.W.E.R. 100 List: You're Closer Than You Think

I've always believed that in everyone's life there are at least 100 people who like, love, and respect you. There are at least 100 people whom you've built a relationship with who would love nothing more than to see you succeed. There are at least 100 people that each have another 100 people in their lives who like, love, and respect them (of which you are one), which means you have access within your close relationships to 10,000 people.

There are two ideas that you must first put out of your mind in leveraging your P.O.W.E.R. 100 list. First, that you *don't have* a list of people you could reach out to. And second, that you don't want to *trouble* them to help you achieve your bigger life vision. Everyone has this list of at least 100 people, and they would profoundly love to help you achieve your goals. Your list could include your friends, your parents' friends, your professors, past bosses, past co-workers, family, people from church, networking chums, and/or workout buddies. You'll soon find that it's easier than you can imagine to build the list.

To begin, open an Excel spreadsheet or a Google Sheets document and create four columns: First Name, Last Name, Email Address, Phone. Begin by populating the list with those closest to you, and fill in the rest as you go. The end goal should be a document with at least 100 names, emails, and phone numbers on it. (The phone number column is nice to have, but not a need-to-have.) I use a Google Sheets file for my P.O.W.E.R. 100 list because it grows on a regular basis, and it's convenient to log in on my phone or laptop and add contacts to the list. My list has grown to nearly 400 people now, who would all be willing to lend a hand should I need one. That assistance might look like an introduction to important contacts, information, physical help, advice, exchange of services, donations to a cause or a crowdfunding campaign, or any number of requests I might make to them.

When crowdfunding the *Broke, Busted & Disgusted* documentary, the first email I sent was to my P.O.W.E.R. 100 list, and it resulted in hundreds of contributions to what would ultimately become a successful $67,000 fundraising effort. Not only did my list financially contribute to the campaign, but dozens upon dozens of them also spread the word on social media, creating an even more viral campaign.

Once the film was completed, I again leveraged my list and asked if anyone had contacts in media licensing and distribution. What bubbled up from that email was a contact in Houston, a relative of a friend's wife, who just so happened to be the person that introduced our film to the folks at CNBC, resulting in a television contract.

There are a couple of keys to leveraging your network effectively. The first is to be relatively sparing with the requests. There is a social capital within your list. I'm careful not to ask too much of my contacts, but I'm more than willing to help them out if they ask. I'm generous with my time when folks on my list ask for advice, coaching, or an introduction to someone I know. My goal is to keep the social capital built with my contacts by sharing key pieces of information, contacts, advice, or wisdom with them throughout the year.

The second key is making sure you're in contact with your P.O.W.E.R. 100 list at least three or four times a year via email. Let them know what you've been up to and inquire whether there's anything you can do for them. This continues to build the social capital you have with them over time. Requests that come out of the blue aren't often responded to, while those that grow accustomed to hearing from you will often reply right away when you ask for help.

The simplest way to send mass emails to your entire P.O.W.E.R. 100 list is to use a service like MailChimp. The service allows you to write one email that automatically populates the name of the recipient and sends the email out to everyone on your Excel or Google Sheets database. You can even use MailChimp to track the open and click-through rates on each email. This way, you'll know who are the most active contacts on your P.O.W.E.R. 100 list. MailChimp is free to use, all the way up to 2,000 contacts.

While my email lists have grown substantially, requiring me to use a different service provider, the emails that I send out to the entire list read something like this:

Dear <firstname>,

Hey, it's been a couple of months since I last reached out— wanted to give you a heads up on what I've been up to and see if there's anything I can do to help you reach your highest goals.

The last couple of months, I've been neck-deep in content projects. One was a video project and the other more written content for a client in the financial space. Both were super rewarding, but I'm looking forward to the coming quarter where I'll be focused on doing more speaking. If you know of anyone looking for a great keynote or breakout speech, please let me know or mention my name. I'll make you look really good!

I'm carving out time this quarter to do more networking as well, not just to expand my circle of friends, but also to help other people achieve their goals. If you have any projects you need or want help with, ping me back and let me know how I can assist. If you have time for breakfast or coffee, I do those things almost every day!

Thanks for being someone I can count on! Have a fantastic rest of the month.

Here's to a bigger life,

Adam

PS: I found this great TED talk you should check out:

You've identified who your P.O.W.E.R. 100 list is, documented their emails, established a MailChimp account, and uploaded the list. Now that you're armed with all of the information from this chapter, here's what you can do with it.

It's time to take at least one of the items from Tenet 3 (Holding a Bigger Vision) and put it in front of your P.O.W.E.R. 100 list to see who might be able to help you get that much closer to it.

In Episode 124 of the Build a Bigger Life podcast, I interviewed Samantha Burmeister, otherwise known as 9to5Nomad. Shortly after Sam's interview, her employer started cutting way back on work-from-home opportunities. It seemed as though her intentions of becoming location independent might not be achievable in the current environment. Sam immediately leveraged her P.O.W.E.R. 100 list and asked about location-independent opportunities that her contacts knew about. A number of replies came back with resources for Sam to investigate, and ultimately she found a number of opportunities to do work that was meaningful to her and could be done from very meaningful places around the globe. Sam's bigger vision, as she shares in the episode, is to travel to every country in the world before she's 50. As things unfold, she may be achieving that big vision far earlier than she had envisioned! All thanks to her P.O.W.E.R. 100 list and simply *asking*.

Now it's your turn.

Tenet 6 is all about leveraging the P.O.W.E.R. of connections to help you achieve the bigger life you desire. What is something, even a reasonably small something, that you could send out to your P.O.W.E.R. 100 list, asking for help? I've found that there is great power in asking, and there are dozens, if not hundreds, of people around you who would love to see you achieve everything you've set your sights on.

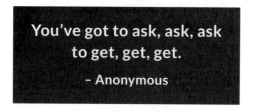

You've got to ask, ask, ask
to get, get, get.

– Anonymous

Tenet 7

Making Money Irrelevant

Of all of the tenets in the manifesto, this one has proven to be the most challenging and the most gratifying.

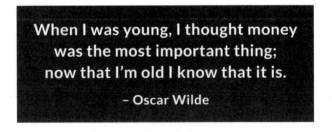

> When I was young, I thought money was the most important thing; now that I'm old I know that it is.
>
> – Oscar Wilde

I want to take you back to your high school graduation. You remember walking across that stage believing that you'd accomplished something amazing and now the world was your oyster. You had no debts, no worries, no obligations... no clue. And then, for most people, their parents sent them off to college to "find themselves," and that's where the programming began.

Oscar Wilde's quote is profound because as young people, we were in school 35 hours a week and didn't have the time to make full-time money, but we had desires (probably instilled from our parents and friends) that required full-time money to afford, though we didn't know that at the time. We just knew that money was important. After all, our parents left every morning to pursue a paycheck, not always pursuing their passion.

It's the way we leave the house and enter the world of school and work that will ultimately start the process of becoming an American consumer in debt. For millions of young people today, they begin their 20s racking up what will become an oppressive amount of debt and corresponding payments. They'll use credit cards because it's too damn easy not to, and the beater of a car their parents gave them will give up the ghost, then they'll have to buy or lease a car. And just like that, Oscar Wilde was right. Now that they're adults, they know money is the most important thing.

It is my firmly held belief that money becomes a central part of most people's lives because they build a big lifestyle thinking money is what creates happiness. If the work they do for the money is what they love, then happiness will more than likely be a by-product.

However, for those who don't love what they do, going to work every day to pay for a lifestyle that's supposed to make them happy can become an eternal grind. Work to live to work to live. Wash, rinse, repeat. Over and over and over...

Building a bigger life is not about working to live or living to work, it's about LOVING your work. It's also about being able to hit the pause button every now and again, just because.

Money irrelevancy is getting to a point where the decisions you make are no longer financially driven. The point where you have a myriad of choices, options, freedom, and flexibility. Do what you love because you love it, not what you have to do to pay the bills.

Money Is Hyper-Relevant Today

As a society, we've made money hyper-relevant, and I've often said that when you truly believe everything you read in magazines or see on TV, the marketers have won. We've stopped thinking for ourselves when it comes to money, our goals, and the quality-of-life.

It's easy to believe in the following when everyone is doing it and quasi-celebrities on TV are telling you these are good things:

- Buying anything on 24 easy monthly installments
- Paying for a car over 7 to 10 years
- Paying off a student loan over 25 years
- Paying 30 years or more on your mortgage

I started questioning all of this about 10 years ago. When I did, everything shifted. It was as if I was Neo in *The Matrix*, and I'd just taken the red pill. What I awakened to was the idea that we are all living in a banker's business model. We tell them how much we need to borrow to buy the things we most "need," and they tell us how much we'll have to pay every month over a certain period of time. We don't question the mechanics of the arrangement. After all, it's been done this way for decades. And in not questioning, we make money hyper-relevant. Because within these agreements is a hidden truth: **A majority of the money you make is no longer yours.**

When my wife and I were first married, we read the book *Smart Couples Finish Rich* by David Bach. It was a turning point for both of us as our financial compasses did not point true north. My wife had grown up in a household that was super frugal by necessity, and as a result, she had mastered couponing and loved having money in savings. My parents were very abundance-focused, and as a result, I appreciated finer things and had a propensity to spend. After reading the book chapter-by-chapter and discussing each one, we got on the same trajectory when it came to money.

At the time, there was another book advertised on the radio entitled *Debt-Free and Prosperous Living* by John Commuta. His book described in great detail how to go about knocking out debts and living a prosperous life. We both agreed that our first challenge as husband and wife was knocking out the entirety of the debt we had accumulated from college, cars, and consumer goods. At the time, Jenn was making about $3,200 in take home pay and I was bringing in about $2,800. We agreed that if we could live on Jenn's income—paying the mortgage, utilities and grocery bill—then my income would be used on a monthly basis to knock out all of our debt.

By living on one income the first two years of our marriage and paying off all other debts (with the exception of our mortgage), we created a discretionary income of nearly $3,000 a month.

This number we began to call our "L" Factor, "L" for Life. If we focused on this number and let it grow over time, it would lead us to a bigger life while affording us plenty of choices and options moving forward.

Your "L" Factor is very simply, **(Income – Expenses) X Time**

When you have consistent and substantial disposable income each month over a period of months, your "L" Factor becomes very real. What you do with that "L" Factor is what determines money irrelevancy.

> **Answer this simple question: If you were digging a foundation for a new home, would it be more efficient with a backhoe or a spoon?**

In the end, the two things you can do with the Life Factor are:

Deleverage—Pay off debts with high monthly payments resulting in higher and higher disposable income (or the ability to quit your job at some point and pursue something more meaningful, fulfilling, etc.). This may mean downsizing your lifestyle to reduce payments. But realize that the quality of your lifestyle may be pushing freedom, flexibility, and other options way out into the future (perhaps even beyond your ability to enjoy them).

Or...

Leverage—Buying assets that generate monthly cash flow allowing you to live a bigger life (and lifestyle as your monthly cash flow grows). That extra discretionary money may be what you need to increase your passive income, to begin that side hustle project, or take a course allowing you to pursue what you've always wanted.

The Pursuit of Financial Freedom

Financial freedom is a simple thing to attain: have more monthly cash flow coming in from passive sources than you have in expenses each month. It's not always easy, but it is a very simple concept.

The reason financial freedom is so elusive to many is they continually increase their expenses and never have an "L" Factor to invest in assets that have a monthly return. The possessions that most people own and consider assets are actually liabilities that pull money from their paychecks every single month. As Robert Kiyosaki so eloquently stated in *Rich Dad Poor Dad*, "Most people believe they have assets, when in fact they have liabilities."

My wife and I lived by a mantra as we paid down our

debts: If you do for two years what most people won't do, you'll do for the rest of your life what most people can't do.

What Do You Do with the "L" Factor to Build a Bigger Life?

This, it seems, is the biggest question for most families that are disciplined enough to have more money at the end of their month. What exactly should I do with this money to make sure it's working most efficiently for me?

For years I believed in the notion that we should have 3 to 6 months' worth of living expenses put away in case of an emergency. In fact, when my wife and I were going through *Smart Couples Finish Rich*, the author encourages couples to get on the same page about how much is needed in savings to feel safe and secure. When I asked my wife what she needed in savings (at the ripe age of 25), her immediate answer was $20,000.

I thought she'd hit the Listerine too hard that morning.

However, once we had our debt taken care of two years later, we had an extra $3,000 in discretionary monthly funds. Six and a half months later there was $20,000 sitting in a money market account collecting interest and allowing my wife to sleep very comfortably at night.

Now, I fully realize that number is either seemingly not attainable for some people, entirely too much to have in savings for others, and/or some will tell me that the money is better invested elsewhere. I don't disagree with any of those reactions. The reality of how much someone should have in savings is entirely up to *that individual and their situation.* If you're gainfully employed and are certain your job is stable, perhaps you need substantially less. If you're self-employed and in a business with fluctuating income, perhaps it should be on the high side. And candidly, it is super dependent on what you decide is the amount you're both comfortable with.

At the time, having an emergency/opportunity fund sitting on the sidelines was helpful for us. We had a couple of job changes and periods of smaller monthly income that were subsidized by that money market account. However, today, because of what I'm about to detail next, I'm less concerned about having a specific amount set aside and more focused on having access to that kind of money, should we need it.

It is my recommendation that putting money away in a separate account is critical if you are on the path of building a bigger life. If nothing else, it becomes the money that you'll live on for a while in the event of a job change or starting a business. In fact, a financial planner friend of mine told me his advice is to put away $10,000 in a money market account just to prove to yourself you can. Ultimately, achieving your version of a bigger life will necessitate making some financial moves. Candidly, having money set aside has never come back to bite me.

With that in mind, the strategy I'm about to outline is intended for people who are disciplined about always spending less than they earn. If you fall into the category of people who make a good income, keep expenses in line, and have money going into savings each month (or money sitting in your checking account at the end of the month), read on... this will change your life.

The Shred Method

Do you know what the two greatest expenses in life are? I ask that question at events all the time and get dramatically different answers. Golf, shoes, kids, wives, purses, and Amazon are all commonly heard.

The answer is ***taxes*** and the ***interest expense on debt***.

When I first discovered this nugget of truth, I dug more into it and found that most people will spend 34% or more of their lifetime income in paying interest. Imagine that... an entire third of your lifetime working hours will be to pay a bank interest for the privilege of spending money that you didn't have to spend at the time.

On top of that, you'll spend somewhere between 80 and 120% in interest on your house over the life of your loan on a 30-year fixed mortgage. Meaning if you buy your home for $200,000, you'll pay between $360,000-$440,000 if you stayed there for 30 years making regular monthly payments.

For me this begged the questions:

What could I do with an extra $200,000 to $400,000 over my lifetime?

What is the best way to eliminate both the interest expense on debt and taxes?

The answer to paying less in taxes is to own a business, invest in real estate, and get really knowledgeable about business entities and advanced tax strategies.

The topic of drastically reducing the interest expense on debt became such a fascinating topic for me that I began to intently study finance. Specifically, how to beat the banks at their own game and make my income (and my "L" Factor) extremely efficient.

Earlier, I mentioned that we live in a banker's business model. By that, I mean we borrow money from banks, and they tell us how much we need to pay over a certain amount of time. If we never question that structure, we continue to pay interest, and the bank continues to rake in profits. The interest that we pay every month is income that we **no longer own**, and therefore is not efficient.

Central to the Shred Method is what you do with the money you have left over at the end of the month. Your goal should be to use it as efficiently as possible to continually own more and more of your income.

Unfortunately, most people do one of three things with the money they have left over at the end of the month:

1) **They blow it.** If you find yourself blowing money like a drunken sailor at the end of the month or right before you get paid again, you won't succeed using this strategy. Whether it's food, clothing, entertainment, or something else, the money you're spending may make you feel good, but it's going to prolong your work to live to work hamster wheel.

2) **They save it.** Not a bad idea necessarily, particularly if you don't have your emergency fund fully

stocked. However, money that sits idly in savings isn't really that efficient either. It's there to make you feel more comfortable (i.e. like a security blanket), but as long as you're still paying interest on debts, it could be deployed more effectively.

3) **They spread it evenly over several debts.** It was John Commuta's book that taught me the error of my ways on this strategy. Sending a little bit to a bunch of debts is like trying to toast a piece of bread with a flashlight. It's going to take you forever.

More Than the Debt Snowball

If you're thinking what I'm about to describe is a debt snowball, you're only half right. The debt snowball philosophy suggests by focusing all of your discretionary income on the smallest of your debts, then moving up the ladder from lowest to highest balance, you'll be out of debt faster. Instead of spreading the income over all the debts (like using a flashlight), you focus the additional money on one debt at a time, paying the minimums on all the others, until the debt is knocked out (like using a blowtorch).

Flat out, this system works. If you're in the middle of your debt snowball, *keep after it!* But it's only half of what you could be doing to knock your debt down even faster.

The Power of a HELOC

The Shred Method is more than just a debt snowball.

To fully utilize what I'm about to share, you'll need either a savings account (emergency/opportunity fund) with $5,000 to $10,000 in it, or you'll need access to a Home Equity Line of Credit (HELOC) with about the same amount available.

A traditional home equity line of credit is obtained from a bank or credit union. It's simply a line of credit that is drawn against the equity in your home. They typically have a monthly payment attached to them, are relatively easy to get (if you have some equity), and most people use them to spend money on their homes. In fact, if you pay close attention to the savvy debt marketers out there, you'll often see or hear commercials about using the equity in your home to take a vacation, buy a boat, or do renovations. All reasonable things to do, but you're playing right into the banker's business model by using the equity in your home and then paying them interest in order to spend it.

Think of your mortgage as a one-way street. When you make a monthly mortgage payment, the money goes in, but it can't come back out again. The bank expects you to pay it every single month as outlined in your mortgage. Essentially, the mortgage agreement says, "If you don't pay, you can't stay." Simple enough.

But the HELOC is more of a two-way street. Money can come out and go back in at any time you like (up to the limit of the line of credit). It's not really advertised this way because financial institutions would rather you use the money from your line of credit and pay it back as slowly as possible (making them the most amount of interest). They want you to think of it as a one-way street as well, but this sucker goes both ways, and we're going to take advantage of that.

So for now, understand that having a HELOC (or access to $5,000 to $10,000 in savings) is central to the Shred Method working. Getting one is relatively easy, and if you haven't borrowed anything from it, then you won't be charged anything monthly. To find out if you qualify for one, check with your local bank or credit union and ask them what is involved in getting one set up. Bottom line—if you have equity in your home, you should have a HELOC.

This Is Like Walking Toe Heel, Toe Heel

Once you have a HELOC (or access to money in a savings account), the next step is what has most people scratching their heads. One client of mine told me it was like being told to walk toe heel, toe heel, when all you've ever done your whole life is walk heel toe, heel toe. The banker's business model has been ingrained in our heads as the only way to handle money, and it's inefficient for the consumer.

In all reality, it's a fairly simple switch once you operate this way for a few months.

For most households, the flow of income looks like this:

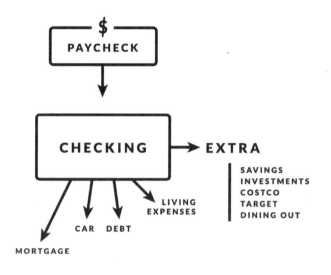

Income comes in once or twice a month, gets deposited into a checking account, and bills are paid from there. The bills are things like a car payment, mortgage or rent, student loan payment, credit card payment, and other living expenses. If there is money left over at the end of the month, it usually goes to savings, investments, paying off debt (inefficiently), or to Target, Costco, or PF Chang's. If there isn't money left over at the end of the month, then it's highly likely that the credit card balances are growing, or certain payments aren't being made.

What we do under the Shred Method is a very minor adjustment. It looks like this:

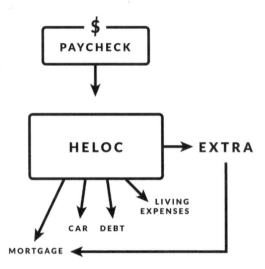

Instead of the income going into a checking account, it is deposited into the HELOC as that will begin to function as your primary checking account. All of the bills that you would normally pay from your checking account are paid from the HELOC exactly in the same manner as before. Car payment(s), student loan payment(s), mortgage, credit card payment(s), and living expenses.

As shown in the first diagram, if your income is $5,000 a month and your expenses are $4,500, there would be $500 left over to be saved, invested, to eliminate debt, or to spend at restaurants and movie theaters.

However, in the second diagram, the $4,500 in expenses and the $5,000 in income stay the same, but there's still room left on the HELOC. This is what gives the Shred

Method its tremendous power to create massive financial freedom. You see, a HELOC can never have a positive balance. It will only ever go as high as zero. And, our goal is actually to *keep* a balance on the HELOC at all times because we're going to deploy it extremely efficiently.

So if $5,000 comes in and $4,500 goes out in expenses, we'd have $500 in the HELOC which I've just said wouldn't be possible (because it would have a positive balance). Our next step is the critical piece of what makes the Shred Method so powerful. You're going to take $750 out of the HELOC and pay down the smallest balance debt.

If you're following along, the HELOC balance will now be -$250. As in you've borrowed $250 *more* than you made that month. This amount will start to generate interest right away, but it's an incredibly insignificant amount compared to what you're saving by paying down debt. Let me illustrate:

Suppose you have a credit card balance of $750 and the minimum payment on it is $35 a month. You've been paying on this for a while, occasionally sending a little bit more every month, but it never feels like you're getting anywhere. (Because you aren't.) Of the $35 you send in, probably $8 to $12 of the payment is actually going to the principal and the rest is going to interest. So if you were to continue the charade of paying off this debt, over the course of a year you'd spend about $250 to $300 in interest.

But if you sent $750 in from the HELOC and paid the debt off immediately, what you'd gain is the $35 that you'd been sending in every month. It is now yours to keep. What you'll pay in interest on the HELOC (assuming a 5% rate) and based on the amount borrowed of $250, is $1.04. [The math looks like this: $250 X .05 = 12.50 / 12 months.] And actually, it would be far less because as soon as you receive your next paycheck, you will pay the amount off.

When you do this on an on-going, bi-weekly or monthly basis, **I can definitively tell you that most people can be completely out of debt in 3 to 9 years *including their home mortgage.***

What we are doing is creating leverage with the amount of money that is left over at the end of the month. We do that by adding a jetpack to it through the HELOC. By using the borrowing power of the HELOC, a vehicle that charges simple interest on small amounts, the money left over at the end of the month turns into significantly more, allowing you to shred debt faster. The faster you shred the debt (especially higher interest compound debt), the more of your income you own. When you start using this against your mortgage, what you'll save is the future interest that you would've paid had you continued playing by the banker's rules.

But It's the Cheapest Money You'll Ever Get

I hear this excuse all the time as to why someone wouldn't pay off their mortgage. Yes, the interest rate on a mortgage, at the time of this writing, is hovering around 4.5%. That is indeed "cheap" money when you consider there are people who paid upwards of 13 to 17% for their home mortgage just a few decades ago. However, it's not only the interest rate that determines how much you'll pay, it's intensely important to look at the balance. If you owe $500,000 on a mortgage at 4.5%, you'll pay nearly $110,000 in interest within the first five years.

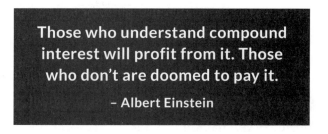

Those who understand compound interest will profit from it. Those who don't are doomed to pay it.

– Albert Einstein

For homeowners with a mortgage, one of the most important things to understand is how your payments are allocated according to the amortization schedule. Because a mortgage is a compound interest vehicle, the lion's share of your payment each month is going to pay interest. On a 30-year fixed mortgage, nearly 90% of the payment is interest for the first several years. That's why when someone lives in a house for only a couple years, they're not likely to get money back at the closing table when they sell. All of the (assumed) equity they have is eaten up by interest, fees, and closing costs.

Mortgages are great things; they allow us to buy homes that we don't have upfront cash for. There is a way to use another vehicle just like a bank would to help pay off your debts (and save you tens or hundreds of thousands in the process). All the while, you'd have access to more and more money via the HELOC, in case you needed it.

Making Money Irrelevant 202: Creating Your Own Bank

Once you've built a substantial amount of equity in your home, you may be questioning what you should do next. After all, many financial professionals (and probably a know-it-all brother-in-law) will tell you that the equity in your home has no internal rate of return. What this means is that whether you own 5% or 95% on your home mortgage, the house is only going to appreciate so much per year (typically around 3 to 4% unless you live on the coasts).

So what do you do with the money that is "sitting idly" in your home equity? Glad you asked.

The answer is to create your own bank. This concept was first introduced to me through a book by R. Nelson Nash called *Becoming Your Own Banker.* What Nash described was an ability to build a high cash value life insurance policy which carried a modest amount of death benefit, but a huge upside potential. He described how you could borrow against the policy (taking your money out), but the policy will still earn dividends as if the money was still there. In the event of your death, the death benefit would cover your loan, and your heirs would receive the rest.

He gave examples in the book from families like the Rockefellers and Walt Disney. Even the Waltons have been named as a family that uses this vehicle to help pass wealth on to the next generation tax-free. Nash's work sparked a whole new breed of insurance agents that know how to structure these policies to their clients' best interests.

So, in digging into this strategy, I interviewed three different individuals on the topic on the Build a Bigger Life podcast. Episode 90 was with Bryan Dewhurst and Phillip Ramsey, collectively known as The Uncommon Wealth Partners, and Episode 23 was with Jake Chesney, an independent agent who sells these policies. All of them extolled the virtues of using this strategy to build tax-free wealth for the future, as well as building a bank for today.

So if this is such a great vehicle, why is it that so few people are utilizing the strategy? The answer, it seems, lies in the fact that most individuals and families don't have access to the kind of money they would need in order to build an effective high-cash-value policy. Or they don't think they have access, but absolutely could.

The policies come in all different shapes and sizes, but to get the most out of a policy, it's best to be able to fund the policy with a significant amount in the first four years. That might mean paying a policy premium of somewhere between $10,000 and $100,000 per year for four years. Again, a significant amount of money for most individuals or families to come up with. The reasoning behind this structure is by front-loading the policy with high premiums, you'll build a high-cash-value policy that earns pretty significant dividends in the first five years. After the fourth year, your premiums back off to a more reasonable amount.

However, if you leverage the power of the Shred Method for a year or two, what you'll find is the amount of equity you have available to you would fully allow you to pay a sizable premium every year. Do that four years in a row, and you're likely to have tens of thousands of dollars in cash value in the policy that you can borrow from at any time.

The cash value in the policy can be used to purchase cars, as down payments on rental homes, to pay for college, or virtually anything else you want to use it for. And because of the way the policy is set up, you get to decide when the payment is made on that loan. Imagine borrowing $40,000 for a new car, but when and how much the payments are on that loan are completely up to you. For the policy to work optimally, you'd want to pay back the loan eventually, but having control over when payments are made and how much the payments are will give you a tremendous advantage.

A Real-Life Example of How This Strategy Works

To give you a more complete picture of this strategy, I'll describe how we used this method in our household to make money irrelevant.

We began using the Shred Method about seven years ago, and in that time, we have nearly paid off our home **twice**. The first three years of using the Shred Method, we paid our $250,000 mortgage down to around $70,000. When we got to $100,000 owed, we actually secured a home equity line of credit large enough to pay off the mortgage with the HELOC. So, in effect, we had no compound interest mortgage, and instead, we had just a simple interest HELOC on the house. At $100,000 borrowed, on a 4% HELOC, our monthly required payment for living in our 3,600 square foot home was $333 a month. At $70,000, it was only $233 a month. Can you see how powerful it is to control your income to that extent? If a traditional mortgage payment on the house is close to $1,700 a month, there's another $1,400 to $1,500 a month that's going to blast away the debt, create more equity, and give you the option of leveraging that on other investments.

With the equity we had in the house, we decided to fully fund a high-cash-value policy that had a premium of $25,000 for four years. That amount would generally be paid out of the HELOC, and the Shred Method would fill the hole back in relatively quickly. After four years of front-loading the policy (called MEC-ing out the policy, an acronym for Modified Endowment Contract), the premium backs down to $5,000 a year. But it also means that around the four- or five-year mark, there is over $100,000 in cash in the policy that's available for you to borrow and use in other ways.

This is where it gets interesting. At the four-year mark, we borrowed around $100,000 from the policy and completely paid off our mortgage. As previously mentioned, the benefit of using a policy this way is we now control when and how much the payments are put back into the policy. The $100,000 we borrowed is effectively a loan from ourselves. While it does accrue interest charges just like a mortgage, the cash value (originally paid in premiums) is still earning dividends that also pay off the loan.

It's worth stating again just in case you missed it: Even when you've borrowed nearly the entire amount from your policy's cash value, it *continues* to earn dividends as if the entire amount is there. What that means to you over time is as the cash value of the policy grows, you can take loans against the policy, and the dividends will pay the loan back. This becomes a source of tax-free income later in life.

To take full advantage of the Shred Method, it's important to work with someone who knows what they're doing, and most importantly, knows what you are doing, in order to help you maximize the use of this strategy. If you trust someone who doesn't fully understand what you're trying to accomplish or structures your policy incorrectly, it won't be nearly as efficient. To learn more about The Shred Method, visit www.TheShredMethod.com.

The F.I.R.E. Movement

Today, there is a new movement brewing among those who have realized that the American dream is actually quite different from what has been sold to us. The movement is called the F.I.R.E. movement and stands for Financially Independent, Retire Early. Those who adopt the mentality of F.I.R.E are living on about 30 to 40% of their income on an annual basis. The rest is used to build passive income through investments in the market, in real estate, and in side-hustle businesses.

Central to the F.I.R.E movement is the idea that it's not necessary to work for 40 years of your life to retire on a third of what you couldn't get by on in the first place. Instead, if you live well within your means for about 10 to 12 years and invest intelligently, you can effectively retire in your 30s or 40s with plenty of money to live out your days.

In Episode 105 of the Build A Bigger Life podcast, I interviewed Scott Rieckens, a F.I.R.E. movement pioneer who moved his young family from San Diego, where the cost of living was skyrocketing, to Bend, Oregon, where the pace and cost of life was more in line with his future goals. Scott detailed the life he and his wife had been living—a beautiful beach town with plenty of high-end restaurants and amenities, a new BMW to drive, and working to pay for this life that they believed they wanted. But in moving to Bend, they now have freedom to spend time with their daughter, a respite from the oppressive costs of maintaining a home in a vacation community, and a chance to reconnect and build the bigger life they've always imagined.

Scott released a documentary called *Playing With Fire,* all about his journey into the F.I.R.E. movement along with others who are practicing this lifestyle choice. Check out www.playingwithfire.co for more information.

These lifestyle changes can be gradual, or you can make the changes overnight. The gradual method is described a bit in my book *30 Days To $1k* available on Amazon. Or, if you want to be extreme, check out those practicing extreme minimalism living in 400-square-foot houses or people who've downsized into tremendous freedom. There is no right or wrong way to do this, as it is 100% personal in the choices and sacrifices you're willing to make.

At a very high level, the way we bank and borrow in this country is what keeps most people chained to their payments. We make bankers and stockholders fortunes, while

Americans work themselves into unhealthy states.

For more information, read books like *Becoming Your Own Banker* by Nelson Nash or *The Joy of Less: A Minimalist Living Guide* by Francine Jay.

Tenet 8

Elimination

At this point in building your bigger life, you've clearly articulated your values, you are learning to see yourself as the architect of your life, you have a bigger vision for your life, you've asked the inner knower bigger questions on how to achieve your goals, you've leveraged the P.O.W.E.R. of connections, and you've started to make money irrelevant. To do those things (and do them well), it's necessary to get rid of some of the things that take up your time.

People ask me occasionally what I mean by building a bigger life, and my natural answer is doing more of what you love to do and less of what you have to do. But I would add that what building a bigger life gives you is more energy. A bigger life = more energy, more vitality, more zest for life, and a clarity of focus and purpose that most people long for.

Tenet 8 is all about elimination because less should be

our focus. Not more.

As a society, we tend towards having more, not having less. There are jaw-dropping statistics about how much mini-storage space there is in the United States—over two billion square feet of it and on the way to three billion. We're renting space to keep junk that no longer has a place in our over-crowded homes. And it's not just costing us money; it costs time, energy, and focus that could be utilized elsewhere in our lives.

Our closets, dressers, and bureaus are overstuffed with clothing that we no longer wear. In fact, a movement was started by Marie Kondo's books and television show encouraging people to keep only what "sparks joy" and get rid of the rest. The fact that a show on purging stuff, organizing efficiently, and loving your less-cluttered space is so popular should shed some light on where we're at as a society. People are intrigued by a less-is-more philosophy because more stuff isn't making them happier. The reality is that elimination is about more than just stuff. We've become overloaded with appointments, to-do lists, meetings, emails, junk mail, subscriptions, and activities.

I've recently read two books that did a great job of explaining the idea of elimination in our lives. The first is *The ONE Thing* by Gary Keller, one of the founders of Keller-Williams realty. When I saw Gary speak at a confer-ence several years ago, it was clear that he was relentlessly passionate about protecting your time. This struck me as rather odd for someone who had grown successful in a service business. For realtors, it seems that their ability and willingness to answer the phone whenever it rings is paramount. However, Gary said if you were to call him, you'd absolutely get his voicemail, and he'd return your call in a day or two. His logic was that you were asking to be scheduled into his day by leaving a voicemail, and depending on the importance of the request, he'd be the one determining if he'd call you back right away or let you hang in the balance.

Keller writes in *The ONE Thing* that he takes the Pareto Principle to the extreme. The Pareto Principle, sometimes known as the 80/20 rule, says that 20% of your activities result in 80% of your productivity. Keller blocks out the 80% of activities that don't impact his life, and instead of just focusing on the 20%, he focuses on the ONE thing that would make the greatest impact.

He advocates asking yourself on a daily basis: What's the ONE thing I can do that can make everything else easier or unnecessary? Asking that question in the mornings has helped me create more focus and priority to my day.

The next book that sits prominently on my desk as a reminder to live this way is *Essentialism* by Greg McKeown. In a nutshell, *Essentialism* is about the disciplined pursuit of less. While the more-is-better philosophy has pervaded the past decade or more, *Essentialism* says less is better. Instead of majoring in minor things, we decide and discipline ourselves to major in major things. And to do that, you have to follow three steps:

1. Explore
2. Eliminate
3. Execute

The entire process is about removing obstacles that are keeping you from living the biggest life possible. The obstacles can be anything, and I'll talk about some of the ones I've removed from my life and how you might do the same. My disclaimer is all of this "life building" stuff is very personal. My ways and means may not fit yours exactly, but my goal is to share with you the mentality I'm using in the process of eliminating and building my own bigger life.

To begin with, I've often heard, "Where attention goes, energy flows, and results show." It may have even been mentioned on the movie *The Secret*. Earl Nightingale, in his audio recording *The Strangest Secret*, put it this way: We become what we think about most of the time.

That caused me to be very mindful of what I was thinking about most of the time. Was it business? My goals? My family? Living at a level ten every day? Or was it the stack of paperwork in the corner of my office that desperately needed attention? The over-stacked closet and chest of drawers with way more shirts than I needed or ever wore? Was it the way-too-numerous-to-answer emails that clogged my inbox? Or the fact that it was a weekend, and we should be cleaning the house?

What I realized throughout this process was that my focus was everywhere. It wasn't focused like a laser beam so much as spread out like a weak flashlight. (And when it comes to focus, focusing on less becomes imperative.)

I found myself paying attention to the fact that when I said yes to someone or something, I was saying no to someone or something else. Every action has an equal and opposite reaction. More time spent sifting and sorting junk meant less time doing what I loved to do. So I got to work figuring out what I didn't want and started eliminating.

In a previous career, I called on mortgage broker offices and wrote loans as a wholesaler through a large bank. One of the clients I called on had an impeccably clean desk. Literally not a pencil was out of place in this guy's office, and when I called him, I noticed how disciplined he was about putting things in the right place and doing it with expert efficiency. His office mate had a desk environment that was the exact opposite—files everywhere, lost paperwork, always searching for pens.

One of the guys was super productive, the other was super social and not terribly productive. He overpromised and always made up for things not happening by smoothing things over with his incredible people skills.

One day, I asked the messier one what was up with the partner's desk. I figured the guy had OCD or some anal-retentive tendencies. What he said stuck with me for years—his partner was so ADD that if there were papers everywhere, he wouldn't get anything done because his mind was so scattered. In effect, he was ruthlessly practicing elimination by focusing on just one thing every time someone came into his office. His focus was always on the task at hand and never on anything else. As it turned out, he also had a small circle of friends and had no desire to increase the friendship circle. After all, that would require additional focus.

There's a concept known as Dunbar's number. It's the

number of relationships that we can legitimately have before it's too many to manage. Believe it or not, the number is 240. At times, I must admit my number of friends and acquaintances has surpassed that and has been a challenge to maintain.

Unfortunately, elimination of some relationships may be critical to you building a bigger life. We all have those friends who light up a room when they walk into it. But there's also the group that can brighten a room by leaving it. Building a bigger life is about spending more time with the former and less with the latter.

I've taken the clean-desk approach in a number of areas of my life. First, my office gets a once-over at least twice a week. That once-over is my chance to get rid of, put away, and generally discard what is occupying my mental focus and energy. Any amount of errant stuff sitting around clutters my mind, distracts my focus, and keeps me from building a bigger life.

In my book *30 Days To $1K*, available on Amazon as a Kindle book and paperback, I talk about getting rid of the clutter and becoming a peddler in the marketplace (the marketplace being Craigslist or Facebook Marketplace). It's a principle of Feng Shui, that too much random stuff becomes an energy-blocker. Clutter itself is defined in Feng Shui terminology as low stagnant blocked energy. I once read that if you're stuck in what to do, clean a drawer. The unfinished tasks around you are draining you of energy. Finishing tasks gives you energy by clearing the low stagnant blockages around you.

Clearing the clutter isn't just about the office space, but

also the home. How many pieces of clothing do you have in your wardrobe or closet that you haven't worn in the past year? Every piece of that is occupying some piece of mental energy for you. While you cram your favorite shirt in the drawer with the dozens of shirts you never wear, you're using up mental energy. What if there were just five shirts in the drawer?

What if you used the one in/one out policy? You can't buy a piece of clothing, a book, a movie, etc. unless you get rid of one first? Sit with that question... does it violate your idea of more is better? If so, that's a good first step.

The last piece of advice is eliminating open time on your calendar. Now bear with me on this one... in the work that I've done in organizations and with leaders, one of the common complaints is their time gets scheduled away in meetings that have little to nothing to do with their primary objectives. And your Outlook or Google calendar is like a vacuum; things will fill the void if the void is there.

So what if you began eliminating time blocks so that no one could reach you during those times? It becomes your singular time to get deep work done, to focus on just one thing, to practice being an essentialist. For me, creating podcasts is a blocked time process. I know that I need an hour to effectively create a solocast, and during that time, nothing else matters. My phone is in airplane mode, the environment I've created is as Feng Shui as I can get it, and I'm racing the clock to do it all within an hour.

Here's the take-away for you in your process of designing the life you most want: less is more. Eliminate for the next week like it's your solitary mission in life to do so. Here are some things to start with:

Your television (or cable)—We haven't had cable in twelve years, and the amount of time that I have with my kids is amazing. Trust me, you don't need it.

Subscriptions—Every time you receive a piece of mail and immediately throw it in the recycle bin, you're using vital mental energy. Save yourself the brain cells; cancel it.

Emails—Once a month, I purge all emails from the system that I somehow have been subscribed to. I limit email production as much as possible and have an assistant that opens and tracks most important emails for me. My personal feeling is that email is an insane waste of productivity but isn't going anywhere.

Clothes—Eliminate clothes from your closet. You'll feel better donating them to a shelter anyway. Seriously, leisure suits aren't coming back, and some of those shirts look ridiculous on you.

Options—And finally, if you want to go to the extreme, a friend of mine eliminated options in his life like where to eat. He has two favorite restaurants, and both are close to work and home for him. If someone wants to meet, they'll meet him at one of these two places and nowhere else. He maintains it's just easier by eliminating options.

This advice obviously is not always one-size-fits-all, but if you take the idea of elimination to heart, I guarantee you'll notice a change in the way you feel, the way you make decisions, how much energy you have, and ultimately, how big your life can actually be.

Tenet 9

Automation

I can hardly wait for automation technology to get to the level demonstrated by Jarvis in the *Iron Man* movies. Imagine saying, "Computer, delete all emails except those that require a response from me," then having the emails read aloud to you in your vehicle. You could transcribe a reply or use canned responses the computer generates from past emails. The amount of time saved will be enormous.

In Tenet 9, you'll learn that to build a bigger life, you have to automate certain facets of your life in both high-tech and low-tech ways. Be prepared, there may be an investment you'll make in creating an automated life or business, but the end goal is always more time to focus on the things that you most value and to enhance your bigger life.

Make no mistake, we're already well on our way to having artificial intelligence all around us, making our lives bigger. You've probably experienced Siri, Alexa, or Google Home as evidence of that, and we're just a few years out from completely autonomous vehicles. It's my prediction that we'll become even more productive as a society as a result.

Merriam-Webster defines "automation" as "automatically controlled operation of an apparatus, process, or system by mechanical or electronic devices that take the place of human labor."

The intent of this chapter is to get you thinking about ways that you can automate certain facets of your life, saving time and mental energy, just as I and other interviewees from the Build A Bigger Life podcast have.

Daily Tasks

I have always hated paying bills. A decade ago, when people still had to sit down and write checks and mail them in, I longed to reach a point where there were only two or three checks to write and that was it. When automated payments became a thing, I celebrated not having to write any more checks.

Today, the bill paying process is exceptionally easier. We've narrowed down our payments to a mortgage and HELOC payment (discussed in Tenet 7), a credit card payment (where literally *everything* is charged), and only two vendors who don't accept credit cards for payment. Paying bills takes less than five minutes and is relatively stress-free.

Think through the tasks you "must" do to get through life:

- Shopping for groceries
- Mowing the lawn
- Dropping off/picking up dry cleaning
- Cleaning the house
- Getting your car serviced

Each of these listed above (and dozens of others) can be automated to the point where human intervention is minimized.

Most large grocery stores now have an online ordering system that allows you to save shopping lists, order from the comfort of your home, and have the groceries delivered. Instacart, founded in 2012, is a company that offers "groceries delivered in as little as an hour." For $99 per year, you can order your goods delivered from retailers like Costco, Walmart, Aldi, Fresh Thyme, Natural Grocers, CVS, local grocery stores, and even Petco. Needed items can even be added on the fly by anyone in the family through the Instacart app. Grocery shopping is the bane of my wife's existence, and by automating the buying and delivery process, her life is significantly bigger.

My biggest frustration used to be mowing the lawn. It was a chore to push the mower, I got sweaty in the heat, and it felt like a giant waste of time. The saving grace is the fact that I love listening to podcasts and that provided an hour of "uninterrupted" listening time. For years, my neighbor has given me grief about mowing my own lawn, telling me it's not worth my time, and I should be focused on higher dollar activities—and he's right! But in doing the math, I was still opposed to paying hundreds of dollars to have a manicured lawn all summer. The solution was to purchase a riding lawn mower that ultimately accomplished two goals:

1. The time to cut the lawn was shaved down to about 25 minutes, and I'm not sweaty from doing it.

2. My boys actually enjoyed mowing because it felt less like a chore and more like driving a go-cart.

The solution ultimately created a small business for my sons, who now use my mower to mow the neighbors' lawns and get paid handsomely to do so. Their business is also my gain—to use the mower I purchased, they have to mow my lawn for free. Boom. Automated.

For the days when they're no longer motivated to mow, I've already decided to purchase a Roomba-esque robotic lawn mower that goes over your yard 24/7 and keeps the grass at a tidy, even length. They're currently around $2,500. But imagine never having to deal with your lawn again!

Automating dry cleaning may not seem like much of a time savings, but the mental energy I expend is now next to nothing. After forgetting about shirts at the dry cleaners for a month or so and finally getting a call letting me know they were soon to be labeled "abandoned," I realized I needed to make a change. There is a house in my neighborhood that has dry cleaning hanging on the front door multiple times a month. I found the company they use and called to find out their process. For 40 cents more per item than what I was previously paying, they'll pick up and deliver clothing with a two- or three-day turnaround. All it takes is an email letting them know you have laundry to collect. No more abandoned shirts, and no more trips to the dry cleaners!

Unless you're Monica Geller from *Friends*, there is little satisfaction in the process of cleaning the house. It had been a bi-weekly occurrence in our home for years, and I always felt like I should've been doing anything else: writing, spending time with my wife and kids, or enjoying the outdoors. Essentially, I felt like cleaning the house was making my life smaller, not bigger. We engaged a cleaning service that came in on the same bi-weekly schedule and immediately life was better. Coming home to a clean space is a wonderful thing. Not getting frustrated with each other about the jobs that one person has to do versus another is worth its weight in gold.

I'm still looking for the perfect automated option for getting my car serviced. A friend of mine who purchases a new car every three years or so has a sweetheart deal with the dealership. They let him know when his car is due for servicing, then schedule a time to pick up his vehicle at work, drop a loaner car in his car's spot, and return it once it's finished. He's a busy executive with a hectic travel schedule, so tasks like car maintenance keep him from living his biggest life. By automating the process, he remains as efficient as possible, and spends his free time investing in his family.

None of these may seem like life-altering tasks, but each and every thing you do means there's something else that you aren't able to do. Every time you say yes, you are also saying no. And for many people, saying yes to the mundane tasks of life means you're saying no to more free time, better relationships, and quite often... more money.

A *New York Times* best-selling author once told me, "If you're still mowing your own lawn or cleaning your own home, you are NOT giving the world your gift."

Business Tasks

One of the smartest things I ever did in business was to hire Molly Rose. She was a recent graduate when I hired her to do some task-level work for me in my business, and over five years, she has evolved into the Business Operations Manager for everything I do.

There are too many individual benefits to mention in regard to Molly's skillsets. But the greatest of all of them is her mentality that *everything needs a process, and most can be automated.*

Molly has automated so many facets of the business including email answering, contracting and invoicing, task management, speaking engagement logistics, podcast scheduling, social media posting, and a host of others.

The lynchpin here is not just having someone with a mind for automation who is willing to learn new tasks, it's literally having someone else in your life who can do some of the things you shouldn't be doing. It's realizing that there are some tasks that feel like minutiae but are essential for your business to operate. When Molly and I first began working together, I'd have invoices that wouldn't get paid until 60 to 90 days after an event. It wasn't that the clients weren't paying; it was that I often overlooked the one critical piece of minutiae that makes a business run: billing.

I was running so fast and staying so busy that I didn't have time to send out invoices, which made it feel like I had to run even harder because the money wasn't coming in. But all of that resolved itself when Molly Rose began to look behind the curtain at all of the manual entry things I was doing that could easily be automated.

Today, my businesses run almost entirely through software that handles each piece automatically. Leads come in through the website. They're put in a funnel, scheduled contact with them is automated, contracts and invoices go out, reminders follow, and payment is recorded. All of it with very little human interaction.

We even automated the process of collaborating together, making the business even simpler. Utilizing Asana.com, a project management tool, we limit the amount of emails back and forth to virtually zero. On our scheduled check-in calls, we blitz through our talking points, questions, and follow-ups, then move on to the highest priority to-dos for the week. Brief check-ins and easy-to-answer questions are done through Voxer, essentially a walkie-talkie app. All of it is engineered to keep us both doing what we're great at and making the biggest difference we can in our respective worlds.

If you're at a point in your business where you aren't sure about hiring an assistant, take the advice of some who have gone before you. The entrepreneurs who have built substantial companies will all tell you to hire someone before you need them. The very act of having someone that you're paying to do tasks will force you to get specific about what tasks you need them to do. And with your free time, you'll now focus your attention on getting things done that actually fire you up and make you money.

Employee Tasks

Even as an employee of someone else, consider outsourcing some of the tasks that require an undue amount of your time and are far less valuable than your salary would suggest. Hiring professionals on Upwork.com is a breeze, and often, you're hiring someone who has been trained at a university in the United States but lives overseas. I hired a PhD-level researcher from the Philippines for $6.00 an hour who had her degree from a prestigious U.S. college. One hundred hours and $600 later, I had the most complete research document you've ever seen on a course that has become an incredible lead magnet for my business.

If hiring someone to do your "work" doesn't pass the sniff test for you, consider hiring someone to run errands, go shopping, buy gifts, pick up laundry, or any number of things that require your time and energy but are below your paygrade. One of my mastermind partners hired a firm called Legs On Lease to do a whole host of things that would've taken him out of his job for hours on end. For $15 to $ 20 an hour, he correctly assumed that the investment in someone else's time and energy would pay dividends on his own time and energy.

We are living in the "gig economy," and as such, there are really talented people who are sitting in their homes willing to do work that used to cost a fortune to get done. Whether it's writing, audio work, video editing, copywriting, graphic design, web services, walking your dog, or even gift buying... someone is out there willing to do the work for you at a fraction of what you think it costs.

Simply put, even being an employee of someone else doesn't necessarily mean that you can't automate or outsource some of the things you do. If doing so builds a bigger life for you, it's worth digging into.

Implementation

While I intended to write a manifesto for my children, what happened as I described the tenets to others is that they became enrolled in the mission. As I previously mentioned, whether you choose one, many, or all of the tenets to apply to your life, you'll notice a substantial change in how you feel and how much bigger your life seems.

The implementation of these ideas is crucial. It's not enough to read this book and think, "Yes, I should do that." You actually have to take action. Here's how to do just that for every tenet:

Tenet 1: Build on a Strong Values Foundation

Download the blueprint at www.BuildABiggerLife.com and do the first exercise. It will lead you through a very simple ten- to fifteen-minute process of determining your top five core values. Write those values on a notecard and keep it with you for the next month. Read it aloud multiple times a day, and whenever you're feeling out of alignment with those values, pay attention! This is where your life could be bigger.

Tenet 2: Seeing Yourself as the Architect

Pay close attention to the language you use when talking about your situation to others. When you hear words and phrases coming out of your mouth that blame your current experiences on others, you're not being the architect. Architects design the lives they want to live; they aren't giving up design duties to others.

Tenet 3: Hold a Bigger Vision

If your life seems small, it's likely you don't have a vision big enough to warrant caring about. Pay no attention to how it's going to happen. There are people figuring out how to launch rockets into space and then landing them vertically back on a landing pad in the middle of the ocean. You can figure out how to achieve your big vision. I have faith in you.

Tenet 4: Ask Bigger Questions

Use the questions in Tenet 4 as well as the expanded list in the Build a Bigger Life Blueprint you downloaded from the website. Spend time with those questions each day. Even one big question at the beginning and the end of the day will make a major difference in your life.

Tenet 5: Trust the Inner Knower

When you go about asking yourself the bigger questions, get really quiet and listen for the answers that will come from the inner knower. If you're not sure how to tap into this part of yourself, download the guided meditation from www.buildabiggerlife.com/recordings. Go through the meditation multiple times if you must. The answers are in there, I promise you.

Tenet 6: Leverage the Power of Connections

Begin building your P.O.W.E.R. 100 list. Whether you know what you're going to request of them or not, it's critical that you have this list when the time is right. There are (probably more than) 100 people in your life who like, love, and respect you enough to help you achieve your big vision.

Tenet 7: Make Money Irrelevant

Your first step is securing a HELOC if you own your home. Even a $10,000 line of credit can make a massive difference. Then, create the biggest "L" factor you can to begin using the Shred Method to own more and more of your income. Check out www.theShredMethod.com for more detailed information.

Tenet 8: Elimination

Start in your closet or a drawer that's jammed full of stuff. Eliminate like your life depends on it. Anything you haven't used or needed in the past six to nine months... toss it. Get really good at ridding yourself of things that no longer add energy to your life, and it will immediately feel bigger.

Tenet 9: Automation

Start with the easiest possible thing to automate that would make a difference in your life. From Tenet 9, this might be grocery shopping, accounting tasks, lawn care, or housework. Decide what one thing you could automate first that would make the greatest difference for you. Then implement!

Again, just reading this book isn't enough. It requires action on your part. We've built a community of life architects in a private Facebook group that is there to provide support, guidance, and a fair amount of celebration as you embrace this philosophy. Join us by searching Life Architects Society on Facebook.

As far as we know, we get one ride on this great, blue ball spinning through the galaxy. As life architects, the life we live is ours to define, and bigger is definitely better!

Please know this: I'm for you, and I'm with you. The world needs you to show up in the way only you can, and no one has greater control over your life than YOU.

Notes

Tenet One:

1. Gross, Scott. (2012, July 5) *The New Millennial Values.* Retrieved from https://www.forbes.com/sites/prospernow/2012/07/05/the-new-millennial-values/#76ca2a07976f, November 18, 2019.

Tenet Two:

1. Eckart, Kim. (2018, June 14) *Study shows how intensive instruction changes brain circuitry in struggling readers.* Retrieved from https://medicalxpress.com/news/2018-06-intensive-brain-circuitry-struggling-readers.html, November 18, 2019.

Tenet Four:

1. Perez, Sarah. (2018, July 31) *U.S. adults now spend nearly 6 hours per day watching video.* Retrieved from https://techcrunch.com/2018/07/31/u-s-adults-now-spend-nearly-6-hours-per-day-watching-video/, November 18, 2019.

Join me at the Build
a Bigger Life Retreat

The Build a Bigger Life Retreat is a 3-day power packed conference with like-minded architects held in beautiful locations around the U.S. You'll spend quality time diving deep into the development materials based on the Manifesto, all the while enjoying the company of others who will inspire you, challenge you, and ultimately become your accountability partners in building a bigger life.

Visit www.buildabiggerlife.com/retreat for more information and to get on the waiting list for an upcoming retreat.